PART ONE: THE OFFICIAL MOTORCYCLE HANDBOOK

Introduction

Motorcycle driving can be an enjoyable, even exciting experience — but it can also be dangerous. As the driver of one of the smallest vehicles on the road, you are more likely to be injured or killed if you are involved in a collision. To avoid collisions and survive, you must learn to drive carefully and safely.

Driver error is the most common cause of traffic collisions. A large percentage of the errors motorcycle drivers make in fatal collisions are due to speeding and losing control. Age also seems to be a factor — many of the motorcycle drivers involved in fatal collisions were under the age of 25.

To help you become a safe and responsible motorcycle driver, Part One of this handbook gives you basic information about safe driving techniques and practices, and Ontario's laws for motorcycle driving. The Official Driver's Handbook must be used along with this handbook.

The Ontario Ministry of Transportation encourages new motorcycle drivers, and those who wish to improve their skills, to take a motorcycle training course. For information about motorcycle driver training, or a course being conducted near you, call your local community college or local Driver Examination Centre.

As you read this handbook, remember it is a guide only. For more detailed information about safe driving, you can read the book Road Worthy, a driving textbook produced by the Ministry of Transportation. For official descriptions of the laws, look in the Highway Traffic Act of Ontario and its Regulations.

Information on how to get licences to drive other types of vehicles is available in Part Two of this handbook, the Official Driver's Handbook, the Official Truck Handbook, the Official Bus Handbook and the Official Air Brake Handbook. To find out how to get these publications, please see pages 149-150.

CONTENTS — Part one

INTRODUCTION   5

1. GETTING YOUR MOTORCYCLE LICENCE   9

What you need to drive a
   motorcycle in Ontario   9
Graduated licensing   10
Graduated licensing
   requirements   11
Level One (Class M1)   11
Level Two (Class M2)   11
Road tests   12
Visitors and new
   Ontario residents   12
New residents from Canada
   the United States and
   Switzerland   13
New residents from
   other areas   13
Could you pass?   14

2. GETTING READY TO DRIVE   15

Get into the right
   frame of mind   15
Avoid drugs and alcohol   16
Stay calm and alert   16
Wear a helmet   17
Wear protective clothing   18
Know your motorcycle   19
Primary controls   19
Secondary controls   22
Do a pre-drive motorcycle check   25
Adjust your mirrors   26
Turn on your headlight   26

3. BASIC MOTORCYCLE DRIVING SKILLS   27

Take a motorcycle
   safety course   27
Getting on the motorcycle   28
Starting your motorcycle   28
Shifting gears   29
Driving along   30
Turning   30
Braking   31
Parking your motorcycle   32

4. SAFE AND RESPONSIBLE DRIVING 33

Driving defensively   33
Seeing   34
Check your mirrors   37
Being seen   38
Being seen at intersections   41
Communicate with
    other drivers   42
Keep a cushion of space
    around you   44
Distance in front   45
Distance to the side   46
Distance behind   48
Keep a safe distance
    from trucks   49
Lane position   50
Changing lanes   54
Lane sharing   54
Lane splitting   54
Passing on the shoulder   54

**5. DEALING WITH PARTICULAR
SITUATIONS**   55

Starting on a hill   55
Vehicles turning left
    in front of you   56
Freeway driving   57
Entering a freeway   57
Changing lanes on
    a freeway   58
Leaving a freeway   58
Driving on dangerous
    surfaces   59
Driving over railroad and
    streetcar tracks   60
Grooves, gratings and
    scraped roads   61
Driving at night   61
Overdriving your headlight   62
Driving in rain   62
Tips for safe driving in fog   64
Driving in fog   65
Driving in cold weather   66

Driving in a group   67
Carrying passengers   68
Carrying cargo   70
Towing a trailer behind
    a motorcycle   70

6. DEALING WITH EMERGENCIES   71

Emergency braking   71
Emergency steering   72
Taking a turn too fast   72
Driving over objects   73
Flying objects   73
Animals on the road   74
What to do if
    a tire blows out   74
What to do if
    the throttle gets stuck   75
What to do in a wobble   75
What to do if a chain breaks   76
What to do if your
    engine seizes   76
Getting off the road   76

7. **KEEPING YOUR MOTORCYCLE ON THE ROAD** — 77

Insuring your motorcycle — 77

Registering your motorcycle — 78

Buying or selling a used motorcycle — 78

Safety Standards Certificate — 79

Maintaining your motorcycle — 80

Accessories and modifications — 81

Choosing a motorcycle safety course — 82

8. **LEVEL ONE ROAD TEST** — 83

9. **LEVEL TWO ROAD TEST** — 87

   I. **Left and right turns** — 88

   II. **Stop intersection** — 93

   III. **Through intersection** — 96

   IV. **Freeway** — 98

   V. **Lane change** — 102

   VI. **Roadside stop** — 103

   VII. **Curve** — 106

   VIII. **Business Section** — 107

   IX. **Residential section** — 109

Motorcycle clubs and associations — 111

PART TWO: OFF-ROAD VEHICLES — 113

CONTENTS — PART TWO — 116

GETTING YOUR MOTORCYCLE LICENCE

This chapter tells you what licence you need to drive a motorcycle in Ontario, whether you are a new driver, a visitor or a new resident in Ontario. If you are applying for your first licence, this chapter explains the graduated licensing system, including the tests you will have to pass and the driving privileges you will have at each licence level.

What you need to drive a motorcycle in Ontario

You must be at least 16 years old and have a valid motorcycle licence (Class M1, M2, or M) to drive a motorcycle in Ontario.

In Ontario, there are 12 different kinds or classes of licences that qualify you to drive different types of vehicles. The class of licence you have must match the type of vehicle you are driving. You need a Class G licence to drive a car, van or small truck. You must have a Class G licence before you can be licensed to drive most other types of vehicles. The only exception is motorcycles. You may get a Class M licence without first getting a Class G licence.

You can get more information on the other classes of licences — A, B, C, D, E, F and G — in the Official Driver's Handbook, the Official Truck Handbook and the Official Bus Handbook. The Official Air Brake Handbook tells you how to qualify to drive a vehicle equipped with air brakes. See pages 149-150 for information on how to get these handbooks.

Some recreational vehicles have special licence requirements. If you plan to drive an off-road vehicle, snowmobile or moped, or pull a trailer behind a motorcycle, read the Off-Road Vehicles section in this handbook.

Graduated licensing

New drivers applying for their first car or motorcycle licence enter Ontario's graduated licensing system. Graduated licensing lets new drivers get driving experience and skills gradually. The two-step licensing process takes at least 20 months to complete.

To apply for a motorcycle licence, you must be at least 16 years old and pass a vision test and a test of your knowledge of the rules of the road and traffic signs. You must also pass a written test of your knowledge of motorcycles. After you pass these tests, you will enter Level One and get a Class M1 licence.

You must pass two road tests to become fully licensed. Passing the first road test lets you move to Level Two (Class M2). Passing the second road test gives you full Class M driving privileges.

The Ministry of Transportation encourages all new drivers to take an approved motorcycle safety course to help learn the proper driving skills and knowledge. This course can be taken in Level One or Level Two and includes a road test. If you pass an approved course, you can reduce the time you must spend at Level Two.

Graduated licensing requirements

Here are the rules you must follow at each level:

Level One (Class M1):

Level One lasts a minimum of 60 days. The M1 licence is valid for 90 days. (It is a good idea to book your Level One road test well ahead to avoid a long delay.)

While at Level One:

- You must not drive if you have been drinking alcohol. Your blood alcohol level must be zero.
- You must drive only during daylight hours — one-half hour before sunrise to one-half hour after sunset.

- You must not drive on roads with speed limits of more than 80 km/h except Highways 11, 17, 61, 69, 71, 101, 102, 144 and 655. (These exceptions are made because some drivers have no other route available to them.)
- You must not carry passengers.

You must pass a road test of your driving skills to move to Level Two. At this time, you will be given a Class M2 licence.

Please note: If you take your Level One road test as part of an approved motorcycle safety course, you must still wait 60 days to move to Level Two. However, the course certificate is valid for only six months. Be sure you take it to a driver examination centre after 60 days but before the six months have passed or you will have to take your road test over again.

Level Two (Class M2):

Level Two lasts a minimum of 22 months. If you pass an approved motorcycle safety course, you can reduce the time spent at Level Two by four months. At this level you have more privileges because of your driving experience. You can drive at night and on any road. However, at Level Two:

- You must not drive if you have been drinking alcohol. Your blood alcohol level must be zero.

After you have completed the time required at Level Two, you may take a road test to qualify for full licence privileges. You must pass this test to get a Class M licence.

Remember: If you take a road test as part of an approved motorcycle safety course, your course certificate is valid for only six months. Be sure you take it to a driver examination centre before the six months have passed or you will have to take your road test over again.

If you have a valid Class M2 or Class M licence, you may also drive Class G vehicles under the conditions that apply to a Class G1 licence. Please see the Official Driver's Handbook for more information on Class G licences.

Road tests

Road tests check your driving skills on the motorcycle and in traffic. You will be tested on your ability to apply the rules of the road and safe driving practices.

The Level One road test deals with basic driving skills. The Level Two road test deals with advanced knowledge and skills that are generally gained with driving experience. Your performance in each of these tests will tell you whether you need more training or practice.

For more information on the Level One and Two road tests, see chapters 8 and 9.

Visitors and new Ontario residents

If you are a visitor to Ontario and want to drive while you are here, you must be at least 16 years old and have a valid motorcycle licence from your own province, state or country. If you are from another country and visiting Ontario for more than three months, you need an International Driver's Permit from your own country. If you do not have an International Driver's Permit, you can apply for an Ontario licence.

If you are a new resident of Ontario and have a valid motorcycle licence from another province or country, you can use that licence for 60 days in Ontario. If you want to continue to drive after 60 days, you must get an Ontario motorcycle licence.

New residents from Canada, the United States and Switzerland

If you are a licensed motorcycle driver with two or more years of driving experience in another Canadian province or territory, the United States, or Switzerland, you may get full Class M licence privileges without taking a knowledge test or any road test. However, you must meet all medical requirements, including a vision test, and show acceptable proof of your previous licence status and driving experience.

If you have less than two years of driving experience, you may get credit for your experience and enter Level Two of the graduated licensing system. Once you have a total of two years driving experience, you may take the Level Two road test to earn full driving privileges.

New residents from other areas

If you are a licensed motorcycle driver from a country other than Canada, the United States, or Switzerland, you must pass a vision test and a test of your knowledge of the rules of the road and traffic signs. You must also pass a written test of your knowledge of motorcycles.

If you have acceptable proof of two or more years of driving experience, you may take the Level Two road test to earn full driving privileges. If you do not pass this road test, you will get a Level One licence and may immediately schedule a Level One road test.

If you have less than two years of driving experience, you will be placed in Level One. However, if you have acceptable proof that you have the driving experience required for Level One, you can immediately schedule a Level One road test to enter Level Two.

A motorcycle licence from another area is considered acceptable proof if it shows you have the driving experience required.

If you do not have acceptable proof of your driving experience, you will start at the beginning of Level One as a new driver.

COULD YOU PASS?

The rest of this handbook gives you information you will need to pass your tests and keep your driving privileges once you get your motorcycle licence.

Here is a sample question that could appear on the written knowledge test:

When a group of motorcyclists is travelling together the safest way to drive is: (choose one)
A. Staggered formation.
B. Four side by side.
C. Three side by side.
D. In a group.

The test may also ask you about:
- knowledge of motorcycle controls
- proper lane position
- steering control of a motorcycle
- motorcycle equipment requirements
- safety helmets
- carrying passengers or cargo
- handling dangerous surfaces
- downshifting of gears
- proper maintenance of your motorcycle
- driving on wet or slippery roads

The road tests will test how well you use your knowledge. You will be tested on:
- starting, stopping and turning
- traffic signs and lights
- passing vehicles and driving in passing lanes
- travelling through controlled and uncontrolled intersections
- entering and exiting freeways
- foreseeing hazardous conditions and being ready for them
- other safe driving practices

Make sure you read this handbook and The Official Driver's Handbook carefully and that you understand the information before you take your tests.

GETTING READY TO DRIVE

This chapter tells you how to get you and your motorcycle ready to drive. This includes being in good physical and mental condition, wearing a helmet and the proper clothing, knowing your motorcycle and its controls and making sure it is safe to drive.

Get into the right frame of mind

Driving a motorcycle is different from driving a car or any other kind of vehicle. As one of the smallest vehicles on the road, it takes your full concentration and attention to remain safe and in control. This means that you need to be in good physical and mental condition. Do not drive when you are sick, injured, tired, upset or impaired in any way. You need to be calm, alert and focused every time you drive.

2

Avoid drugs and alcohol

Drinking alcohol increases your chances of having a collision. Alcohol can begin to affect your ability to handle your motorcycle safely at blood alcohol levels far below the legal limit. Your balance, steering, speed control and distance perception may be off. Because alcohol also clouds your judgment, you may not recognize these symptoms of impairment until it is too late.

Besides alcohol, almost any drug can affect your ability to drive a motorcycle safely. This includes illegal and prescription drugs. It even includes non-prescription drugs such as cold tablets or allergy pills. These drugs can leave you weak, dizzy or drowsy. Make sure you know the effects of any drug before you drive. If you feel dizzy or weak while driving, stop and wait until you feel normal.

Stay calm and alert

Do not drive when you are tired. You might fall asleep while driving, risking your own life and the lives of others on the road. Even if you do not fall asleep, fatigue affects your ability to perceive and react to emergencies. Your thinking slows down and you miss seeing things. In an emergency, you may make the wrong decision or you may not make the right one fast enough.

It is also important not to drive when you are upset or angry. Strong emotions can reduce your ability to think and react quickly. Be especially careful not to fall victim to road rage. In an argument with a car, a motorcycle will almost always lose. Stay calm and move away from the situation as quickly as possible.

Wear a helmet

A helmet is the most important motorcycle accessory you can have. Wearing a helmet can protect you from serious head injury. **Ontario law says you and your passenger must wear approved helmets with the chinstrap securely fastened every time you drive.**

An approved helmet is one that meets standards approved for use in Ontario. It must have a strong chin strap and fastener and be in good condition. Even approved helmets come in a variety of styles and prices. It is important to choose one that is well constructed and will protect you. A full-faced helmet offers the best protection and the most comfort.

Make sure your helmet fits snugly and does not slide around on your head. Always keep the strap securely fastened. Studies of motorcycle collisions show that a loose helmet will come off in a collision.

Besides protecting you from head injury, a helmet can make you more comfortable when driving because it reduces the noise of the road and keeps the wind, bugs and other debris from blowing in your face.

Wear protective clothing

Protective clothing can help protect
you from injury in a fall or collision
and from the impact of wind, rain,
insects, stones and debris. It can also
help reduce fatigue by keeping you
comfortable in bad weather. Bright
colours and reflective items, such as
a safety vest, make you more visible
to other drivers on the road.

Wear a jacket and pants that
cover your arms and legs completely,
even in warm weather. Leather offers
the best protection, but riding suits
made of special synthetic materials,
can also give you a lot of protection.

Your clothes should fit snugly
enough to keep from flapping but
still let you move freely. Consider
wearing protective equipment such
as back protectors, kidney belts and
body armour as inserts in your protective clothing.

In cold or wet weather, your
clothes should keep you warm and
dry as well as protect you from
injury. Driving for long periods in
cold weather can cause severe chill
and fatigue. Rain suits should be one
piece and brightly-coloured. Those
not designed for motorcycle use may
balloon out and allow wind and
water to enter when driving at freeway speeds. A winter jacket should
resist wind and fit snugly at neck,
wrists and waist. Layer your clothes
for extra warmth and protection.

Choose boots that are sturdy and
high enough to protect your ankles.
Soles should be made of hard,
durable material that will grip the
pavement when you are stopped.
Heels should be short so they will
not catch on rough surfaces. Avoid
shoes with rings or laces that may
catch on the motorcycle's controls.

Gloves are also important in both
cold and warm weather. They give
you a better hold on the handgrips
and controls. Gauntlet gloves that
extend over your wrists are recom-
mended because they protect your
wrists as well as your fingers and
knuckles. Look for sturdy leather
gloves designed for motorcycle use.

Know your motorcycle

The first step in learning to drive a motorcycle is to learn where the controls are and what they do. Motorcycles are designed so that all the controls are within quick reach of your hands and feet. However, the same control may not be in the same place on all motorcycles. Become familiar with **your** vehicle's controls. Check the owner's manual for the exact location and precise method of operation of all controls.

You need to know the controls well enough that you can reach them without taking your eyes off the road. With practice, you will be able to operate all controls by reflex. This automatic response is required before you can begin to drive in traffic.

Primary controls

The following six controls are the most important controls you will use to operate your motorcycle:

1. **Handlebars**
2. **Throttle**
3. **Front brake lever**
4. **Rear brake lever**
5. **Clutch lever**
6. **Shift lever**

This illustration is intended only as a guide. Controls and their positions may be different on your vehicle.

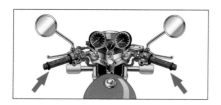

1. Handlebars.
These are the two bars you hold to control the motorcycle's direction. Many of the other controls are grouped on or around the handlebars.

2. Throttle.
Twist the right hand-grip to operate the throttle. This controls the motorcycle's speed by controlling the flow of fuel to the engine. To speed up, twist the throttle toward you. To slow down, twist it away from you. The throttle should spring back completely to the idle position when you let go.

3. Front brake lever.
The front brake lever is on the right handlebar in front of the throttle. You squeeze the lever toward the hand-grip to apply the brake to the front wheel. Use the front and rear brakes together.

4. Rear brake lever.
The rear brake lever is near the right footrest. Press your foot on the lever to apply the brake to the rear wheel. Use the front and rear brakes together. Note: Although the engine will act as a brake when you gear down or reduce throttle, your brake lights will not turn on and other drivers may not know you are slowing down. Always apply your brakes as a signal to others that you are slowing down.

5. Clutch lever.
The clutch lever is on the left handlebar. It controls the clutch and is used to help shift gears. Squeeze the lever toward the handgrip to disengage the clutch; release it to engage the clutch. Whenever you change gears, you must first disengage the clutch. Try to co-ordinate the movements of clutch and throttle to change gears smoothly.

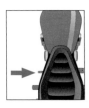

6. Shift lever.
The shift lever is near the left footrest. It shifts the transmission's gears. The shift lever should only be used when the clutch is disengaged. Select the gear you need by lifting or pressing the lever with your foot. Most motorcycles have five or six forward gears and a neutral position. Always start and shut off your motorcycle in neutral.

Secondary controls

There are a number of secondary controls that you will need to use sto operate a motorcycle effectively. Here are some of the most important ones:

7. **Speedometer**

8. **Tachometer**

9. **Indicator lights**

10. **Ignition switch**

11. **Starter**

12. **Choke**

13. **Engine kill switch**

14. **Fuel supply valve**

15. **Turn signals switch**

16. **Horn button**

17. **Light switches**

18. **Stands**

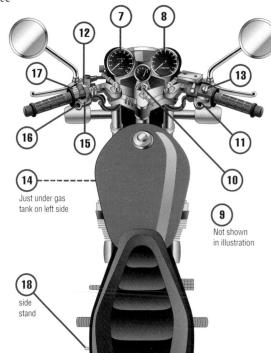

Just under gas tank on left side

9 Not shown in illustration

14

18 side stand

7. Speedometer. The speedometer shows the speed you are driving in kilometres per hour (km/h) or miles per hour.

8. Tachometer. The tachometer shows the number of revolutions your engine is turning per minute (rpm). A red line shows the maximum rpm that is safe for the engine.

This illustration is intended only as a guide. Controls and their positions may be different on your vehicle.

9. Indicator lights.
The highbeam light glows red or blue when the highbeam headlight is on. The neutral light glows green when the transmission is in neutral gear. And the turn signal light flashes yellow when the left or right turn signal is on.

10. Ignition switch.
The ignition switch turns the ignition system on and off. The ignition switch is separate from the starter; you do not turn the key to start a motorcycle like you do a car. Ignition switches have 'on' and 'off' positions and some also have 'lights', 'lock' and 'park' positions.

11. Starter.
Most motorcycles have electric starters. To start, make sure your motorcycle is in neutral and that the clutch is depressed. Push the starter button on the right handlebar near the throttle. Some motorcycles have a kick-start lever, usually above the right footrest. It must be unfolded and kicked downward to start the motorcycle.

12. Choke.
This is a lever or knob, usually on the handlebars, that is used to help start the motorcycle by adjusting the mixture of gasoline and air supplied to the engine. It is used when starting a cold engine.

13. Engine kill switch.
The engine kill switch is used in an emergency to stop the engine quickly. It may also be used to turn off the engine after a normal stop, but be sure to turn off the ignition switch as well. The engine will not start when the kill switch is in the 'off' position.

14. Fuel supply valve.
The fuel supply valve, or petcock, controls the flow of gasoline to the engine. When the motorcycle is not in use, the valve should be turned off to avoid a fire hazard. The fuel tank has a reserve supply in case the main section runs dry. To release the reserve fuel, you must turn the valve to reserve.

15. **Turn signals switch.**
Many motorcycle turn signals do not automatically switch off after a turn is completed. You must manually switch off the signal after each turn or lane change. Forgetting to turn off your signal is as dangerous as not signalling in the first place because it may cause other drivers to pull out or turn in front of you.

16. Horn button. Your motorcycle must have a horn that works. Most horns are operated by pushing a button with your thumb.

17. Light switches. On most modern motorcycles, the headlight and tail light come on automatically when the ignition is switched on and the engine is running. The switch to turn the headlight from lowbeam to highbeam is usually on the left handlebar and operated by the thumb.

18. Stands. A kickstand or centrestand holds a motorcycle upright when it is parked. Some larger motorcycles have both. A kickstand extends from the left side of the motorcycle and the motorcycle leans against it. A centrestand is attached underneath the centre of the motorcycle frame and holds the motorcycle upright. Stands are operated by spring mechanisms and should only be used on a hard surface. Always make sure to completely raise your stands before driving away.

DO A PRE-DRIVE MOTORCYCLE CHECK

Motorcycles require more attention and upkeep than cars. And the consequences of something going wrong are much more severe on a motorcycle. That is why you should always check the condition of any motorcycle before you begin to drive. Here are the things you should check every time you drive:

☐ **Tires**. The proper tires are important for good traction, mileage and safety. Check:
- **Pressure**. Proper tire pressure means safer driving and longer lasting tires. Use an air pressure gauge to check the pressure when the tires are cold. If you do not know what your tire pressure should be, check the owner's manual or check with the manufacturer.
- **Tread**. Worn or uneven tread can make the motorcycle skid, particularly on wet pavement.
- **Damage**. Check for cuts or nails stuck in the tread. Also, check for wear, bulges or cracking. A blowout on a motorcycle can be extremely dangerous.

☐ **Controls**. Make sure all levers, pedals and switches are in good condition and operate properly. They should spring back to the original position when you let go.

☐ **Brakes**. Try the front and rear brakes one at a time. Make sure each one holds the motorcycle when it is fully applied.

☐ **Chassis**. Check for loose bolts.

☐ **Cables**. Check for kinks, binding or broken strands.

☐ **Lights**. The headlight must shine a white light. The rear or tail light must be red. A white light must shine on the licence plate. Keep your lights clean and check that all are working before you drive away.

☐ **Fuel and oil levels**.

☐ **Stands**. Check springs.

Adjust your mirrors

Clean and adjust both mirrors before you start. It is dangerous to try to adjust a mirror while driving. Swing mirrors outward far enough to see around your own body. Adjust each mirror so that it lets you see about half the lane behind you and as much of the lane beside you as possible. Reduce your blind spot as much as possible. Remember that mirrors are not a substitute for looking over your shoulder.

Turn on your headlight

The headlight and tail light of modern motorcycles come on automatically when the motorcycle is turned on. If you drive an older motorcycle with a manual headlight and tail light, remember to turn them on at all times, even in daylight. This improves your chance of being seen by other drivers.

BASIC MOTORCYCLE DRIVING SKILLS

This chapter tells you about the basic skills you need to drive a motorcycle. Controlling your motorcycle means being able to make it go exactly where you want and at the correct speed. It will take practice and experience to master the basic skills of starting, steering, turning, shifting gears and stopping. Practice off the road, in a parking lot or other spot away from traffic, until you can perform all the manoeuvres safely and confidently.

Take a motorcycle safety course

The best way to learn proper motorcycle driving techniques right from the start is to take a motorcycle safety course. You will learn good driving habits from trained instructors, increasing your chances of a safe and enjoyable motorcycle driving experience. For more information on how to find a motorcycle safety course and what you will learn, see page 82.

3

Getting on the motorcycle

Begin by making sure your motorcycle is not too heavy or large for you to drive comfortably. Sitting on the seat, you should be able to place your feet flat on the ground.

If your motorcycle has a kickstand, mount the motorcycle from the left side and straighten it with the handlebars. With the motorcycle balanced, use your left heel to kick the stand up and out of the way.

If your motorcycle is resting on a centrestand, mount the bike and gently rock the motorcycle forward until it rolls off the stand. The centrestand will spring into the up position. Stop the motorcycle from continuing to roll forward by applying the front brake.

Always make sure to completely raise your kickstand and centrestand before driving away.

Starting your motorcycle

Depending on the age and model of your motorcycle, the starting procedure may vary. Generally, you start a motorcycle by turning the ignition switch on and making sure the engine kill switch is not in the 'off' position. This can happen by accident, so it is always a good idea to check.

Shift your transmission into neutral. Set your choke as required. (How you do this will depend on whether your engine is cold, as well as the individual characteristics of your motorcycle.) Pull in the clutch and press the starter button. Release the button as soon as you hear the engine fire. If your motorcycle has a kick starter instead of an electric starter, you will need to unfold the lever, usually above the right footrest, and kick it downward to start the motorcycle.

Once the engine is going, shift into first gear and with your feet still on the ground, slowly ease the clutch lever out until the motorcycle begins to move forward. Raise your feet and continue to ease up on the clutch, applying the throttle to give the engine enough fuel not to stall.

Shifting gears

You need to shift gears as you increase and decrease engine speed — shift up when driving faster and shift down when slowing.

The purpose of the gears in a motorcycle transmission is to match the engine's speed (measured by the tachometer) with the motorcycle's speed (measured by the speedometer). The proper gear will also provide power for the motorcycle to accelerate if necessary.

Learning to co-ordinate the movements of the clutch and throttle to change gears smoothly is a critically important part of driving. Make sure you can accelerate and decelerate smoothly before you attempt to drive in traffic.

To shift up, twist the throttle as you pull in the clutch. Move the shift lever up with your toe until it stops. When you can hear and feel the gear engage, ease off on the clutch and slowly twist the throttle back up to speed.

It is more difficult to downshift smoothly than to shift up. You must twist the throttle slightly to increase engine speed as you downshift with the clutch pulled in. If you do not apply enough throttle, the motorcycle may jerk when you release the clutch. To avoid a rear wheel skid, downshift when the engine speed is lower than the motorcycle's speed.

Do not shift gears while you are turning. A rough, jerky downshift can cause the rear wheel to lock, resulting in a skid. Applying too much power can cause the rear tire to lose traction, also resulting in a skid. It is best to shift gears before entering a turn.

Remember, you shift up when the engine is turning too fast for the motorcycle's speed or to increase speed and you downshift when the engine is turning too slowly or you want to slow down.

Driving along

Steering a motorcycle is very different from driving a car. To make a motorcycle go in the direction you want, you must 'countersteer'. You do this by turning the handlebars in the direction opposite to where you want to go.

When driving along, your body posture should be fairly straight. Sit close enough to the handlebars to reach them with your arms slightly bent so that you can turn the handlebars without having to stretch. Hold the handgrips firmly enough that you will not lose your grip if the motorcycle bounces. Drive with your wrists low to keep you from increasing your speed by mistake. Hold your knees firmly against the gas tank for comfort and better control. Keep your feet firmly on the footrests. Do not drag your foot along the ground. Keep your toes up so they do not get caught between the road surface and the footrest.

Turning

You need to be extra careful when turning or changing lanes on a motorcycle. The only way to learn how to make good, precise turns is to practice.

Slow down before entering a turn. Approach turns with extra caution until you learn to judge how fast you can actually take a turn. If you cannot hold a turn, you may end up crossing into another lane of traffic or going off the road. If you brake too hard when turning, you may skid out of control.

Check your mirrors and over your shoulder to be sure the way is clear and signal well in advance to alert other drivers that you intend to turn or change lanes. Then, lean with the motorcycle into the turn. The sharper the turn and the faster your speed, the more you lean. Look well ahead in your turn. Practise keeping your head upright and facing into the turn. Remember, slow down before you begin to turn. And speed up to come out of the turn. To keep control of your steering, avoid braking in the turn.

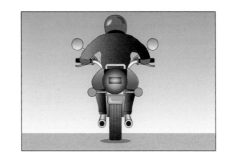

Braking

You need to use both brakes to slow down and stop effectively. The front brake is the more important of the two brakes; it provides about three-quarters of your stopping power. Be careful not to apply the brakes too hard; you may lock up your tires and skid.

Here are some tips for braking:
- Use all your fingers to pull the front brake lever smoothly.
- Use both brakes every time you slow down or stop.
- Always apply both brakes at the same time.
- Do all your braking before you enter a turn.

You can also slow down your motorcycle by downshifting or reducing throttle. However, your brake lights will not turn on when you do this so other drivers may not know you are slowing down. Always apply your brakes as a signal to others that you are slowing down.

Parking your motorcycle

When parking your motorcycle, use your foot to push the kickstand down. Carefully lean the motorcycle to the left to rest on the kickstand.

If your motorcycle has a centre-stand, follow these steps to park it:

1. Stand beside the left side of the bike and hold onto both handgrips.
2. Using your right foot, lower the centrestand until you feel it touch the ground.
3. Balance the motorcycle upright and use one hand to grasp the frame under the saddle.
4. With your right foot securely placed on the centrestand, push down and back on the stand with your foot while pulling the motorcycle back with your arms. The motorcycle should roll up onto the centrestand.

SAFE AND RESPONSIBLE DRIVING

This chapter tells you about the most important principles of safe and responsible driving. These include seeing and being seen, clearly communicating with other drivers, keeping a cushion of space around your motorcycle for safety and positioning yourself in the best possible spot on the road.

Driving defensively

Driving a motorcycle in traffic is more dangerous than driving a car or truck. That is why it is so important to learn the basic skills of driving before you attempt driving in traffic. You will need to focus all your attention on what you are seeing and hearing and then judging what is going to happen next. This is called defensive or strategic driving. Defensive driving is based on three ideas: visibility — seeing and being seen — communication and space.

Seeing

The best way to avoid trouble is to see it coming. Skilled drivers have very few surprises on the road because they see and understand possible problems before getting to them. Learn to look far ahead of where you are driving. In the city, look one-half to one full block ahead. On the freeway, look as far ahead as you can see. Looking well ahead gives you time to adjust to problems. It also helps you to avoid panic stops or sudden swerves that can cause even more trouble.

Follow these steps to develop driver awareness:

- Keep your eyes constantly moving, scanning the road ahead, beside and behind. Do not look at one place for more than two seconds; trouble could be developing in one place while you are staring at another.
- Look ahead as far as you can see. Look beyond the vehicle in front of you for others that are stopping or turning ahead.
- Check the roadside. Watch for vehicles that may leave the curb or enter from side streets or driveways.

Sometimes you cannot see an area because a bridge or truck blocks your view. Good drivers have good imaginations. Ask yourself what might be there that you cannot see yet. Remember, what you cannot see, **can** hurt you.

When looking ahead and scanning the road, check the surface of the road for slippery spots, bumps, broken pavement, loose gravel, wet leaves or objects lying in the road. When driving in winter, be alert for ice and snow patches. Learn to see these spots well ahead so you do not have to look down at the road surface.

In some situations, you can put your motorcycle in a position to see things that other drivers cannot. For example, in a blind curve, where you cannot see all the way around the curve, move to the side of the lane where you can see as much as possible of the road ahead.

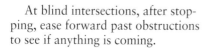

At blind intersections, after stopping, ease forward past obstructions to see if anything is coming.

When you are parked or stopped at the side of the road and want to join traffic on the road, angle your motorcycle across the road so that you can see in both directions.

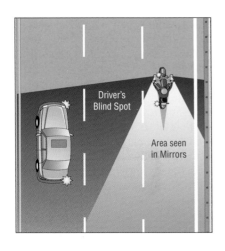

Driver's Blind Spot

Area seen in Mirrors

Check your mirrors

Check your mirrors every five to seven seconds to keep track of traffic coming up behind you. You should have a good picture in your mind of what is behind so someone passing you will not surprise you. You also need to know so you can stop quickly or swerve if any emergency develops in front of you.

It is especially important to check your mirrors in the following situations:

- **Before you have to slow down or stop suddenly or when you are stopped at an intersection.** If the driver behind you is not paying attention, she or he may be dangerously close before noticing you are there. Be prepared to get out of the way.

- **Before you make a turn.** Check vehicles behind you when you plan to slow down and turn. Remember to use your brake lights to signal that you are slowing down. (Gearing down does not activate your brake lights.) If drivers behind you do not appear to be aware that you are turning, it may be safer to continue going straight.
- **Before you change lanes.** Make sure no one is trying to pass you.

Remember that mirrors do not give the whole traffic picture. There is an area on each side of your motorcycle that you cannot see in your mirror. You may not see people or vehicles when they are in these blind spots. Always turn your head and check over your shoulder before you turn or change lanes.

Being seen

You cannot assume that other drivers see you. Drivers that have collided with motorcycles often say they did not see the motorcycle until it was too late.

A motorcycle is more difficult to see than other vehicles. Your profile is smaller from most angles. Even if you are seen, your speed or distance from other vehicles may be misjudged. If a driver does not see you, she or he may pull out or turn in front of you or cut you off. Always ask yourself if the other driver sees you.

Remember, even when other drivers see you, you may be hit if they misjudge your speed, are aggressive or impaired or just careless. Be alert and try to anticipate what other drivers are likely to do.

While your motorcycle's headlight and tail light help to make you visible, there are a number of other things you can do:

- **Wear brightly-coloured clothing and helmet.** This will help make you more visible during the day, especially from angles where your headlight cannot be seen. Yellow, orange, red and other bright colours are highly visible. Black and dark colours are not. Think about wearing a reflective vest, especially at night. Consider adding reflective tape to your helmet, clothing and motorcycle. In the rain, wear reflective rainwear.

- **Slow down when driving at night in front of a group of vehicles.** When you are driving in traffic with other headlights behind you, a driver ahead may not be able to pick out your single light from all the lights behind you. This problem is especially bad when the roads are wet because of lights reflecting off the road surface.

- **Think about your lane position.** Sometimes you can make yourself more visible by moving from one side of the lane to the other or by changing lanes when appropriate.

Do not drive in another driver's blind spot and do not let another vehicle drive in your blind spot. Drop back or pass the other driver. When you pass another vehicle, get through the blind spot as soon as you can. Approach cautiously, but once you are alongside, get by quickly. As a general rule, if you can see a driver in his or her mirror, the driver can see you.

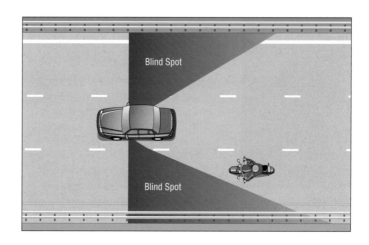

Being seen at intersections

Most collisions between motorcycles and other vehicles happen at intersections. Drivers often have a hard time seeing a motorcycle coming toward them. A vehicle may make a left turn across your path or pull out from a side street. These are the two leading causes of motorcycle collisions at intersections. To cut down your chances of being hit, follow these steps:

- **Approach slowly**. If a driver does pull out suddenly, your chances of making a quick stop or a quick turn are better if you are going slowly.

- **Move as far away as you can from the other vehicle**. If the vehicle is on your right, move to the left. For a vehicle on your left or an oncoming vehicle with a left turn signal on, move to the right.

- **Move away from things that could block the other driver's view**. When you approach an intersection with a vehicle waiting to pull out, move toward the centre of the road so that you are in the other driver's line of sight.

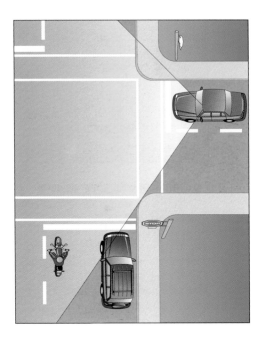

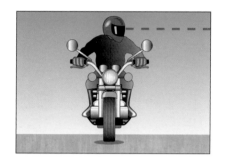

Communicate with other drivers

In addition to seeing and being seen, it is important to communicate with other drivers to make sure they see you and know what you are doing. Make eye contact with other drivers. Check over your shoulder often to make sure other drivers are not crowding you.

Be ready to use your horn before you pass a vehicle or approach a driveway or intersection where a vehicle may pull out in front of you. You can also use your horn before passing a vehicle you think might move into your lane. Watch for situations such as a driver in the lane next to you is coming up behind a vehicle; a parked car with someone in it; or someone walking or riding a bicycle on the road.

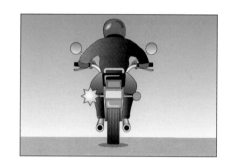

Use your signals to communicate. A driver behind you is more likely to understand your turn signal than your tail light. Use your turn signals even when what you plan to do is obvious. For example, if you use your signals on a freeway entrance ramp, it is more likely that vehicles on the freeway will see you and make room for you. Also, signal whenever you change lanes whether someone else is around or not. It is when you do not see the other vehicle that your signals are most important.

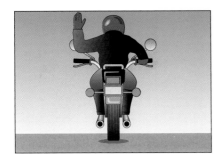

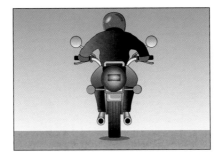

Remember to turn your signal off after you have completed your turn or lane change. It can be as dangerous to forget to turn a signal off as it is to forget to turn it on. A driver may think you plan to turn and pull into your path. Check your instrument panel to see if you have left a signal on. (If you have an older model motorcycle that did not come with turn signals, use the standard hand and arm signals. See the Official Driver's Handbook for a description.)

Tap the brake pedal lightly to flash your brake light before you slow down. This warns drivers behind you that you are going to slow down. This is especially important when you are being followed too closely, when you are making a tight turn off a high-speed road, or when you are slowing down or turning where others may not expect it. Also, keep your foot on the brake, day or night, when stopped for a stop sign or traffic signal.

Keep a cushion of space around you

The best protection you can have as a motorcycle driver is distance — distance between you and other drivers. This gives you time to react to trouble and gives you some place to go.

Always leave a cushion of space around your vehicle to let other drivers see you and to avoid a collision. Keep alert for all other traffic, including vehicles in front, behind, coming toward you and approaching from the side, as well as those you are passing and any that are passing you.

It is important to remember that motorcycles, because they weigh less than most other vehicles on the road, are able to stop and accelerate faster than other vehicles. Keep in mind when deciding how much space to leave around you that other drivers may need much more space to stop than you do.

Distance in front

Always keep at least a two-second distance behind the vehicle in front of you. This gives you time to react if something happens ahead. It also gives you a better view of things in the road, such as potholes, slippery spots, chunks of tire tread or debris. If conditions are less than ideal, such as in bad weather, leave even more space.

To give yourself a two-second space, follow these steps:
1. Pick a marker on the road ahead, such as a road sign or hydro pole.
2. When the rear of the vehicle ahead passes the marker, count "one thousand and one, one thousand and two".
3. When you reach the marker, stop counting. If you reach the marker before you count "one thousand and two", you are following too closely.

2 Seconds or More

When you stop behind another vehicle, leave enough space to pull out and pass without having to back up — about one motorcycle length. If the vehicle in front is large, leave more space. Leaving this space protects you in three ways: it lets you pull around the vehicle in front if it stalls; it helps prevent you from being pushed into the vehicle ahead if you are hit from behind; and it reduces the risk of collision if the vehicle ahead rolls backward or backs up.

Distance to the side

On a motorcycle, you have the ability to change your position within the lane to increase your distance from other vehicles. You should do this as traffic conditions change.

Try to keep a space on both sides of your motorcycle. Do not drive beside other vehicles if you can avoid it. A vehicle in the next lane could move into your lane without warning. Vehicles in the next lane also block your escape if you run into danger in your lane. Drop back or speed up until you find a place that is clear on both sides. And avoid driving in the blind spots of other vehicles.

Here are some of the conditions that require changes in lane position:

- **Passing vehicles**. When you are being passed by an oncoming vehicle or from behind, move toward the centre of the lane. Avoid being closer to a passing vehicle than you have to be; a slight mistake by either driver could cause a sideswipe.

- **Parked vehicles.** By staying to the left side of the lane, you can avoid the dangers of opening doors, drivers getting out of vehicles or people stepping from between vehicles.
- **Vehicles pulling out.** When pulling out into traffic, other drivers often take a quick look behind them and fail to see a motorcycle. Vehicles making U-turns are a particular danger. If you see a vehicle pulling out, approach with caution.

Distance behind

Many drivers complain about 'tail-gaters' — people who follow others too closely. If someone is following you too closely, change lanes and let the tailgater pass. If a driver still follows you too closely, increase the distance between you and the vehicle ahead. This gives you and the tail-gater more time to react in an emergency. Then, when the way is clear to pass safely, slow down so the tail-gater can pass.

Keep a safe distance from trucks

Avoid driving behind trucks. In addition to blocking your vision and blowing debris in your face, trucks create air turbulence that can seriously affect your control, pushing your motorcycle all over the road. Stay well back to avoid this.

Passing a truck on a motorcycle is difficult and can be dangerous. If you must pass one, try to relax and work with the air turbulence. After you pass through the first blast of turbulent air coming off the back of the truck, you will feel a stream of air either pulling you toward the truck or pushing you away from it, depending on wind direction. Lean away from the truck if the wind is pulling you toward it, or lean toward the truck if you are being pushed away. More turbulence will be waiting for you coming off the front of the truck. Lean into this wind as you pass in front of the truck.

Lane position

On a motorcycle, you do not have the protection of a vehicle around you, so you have to make your own protection. This is done by positioning your motorcycle in the best possible spot on the road.

Depending on traffic and road conditions, the best position in the lane is usually a little to the left or right of the centre of the lane where the tires of a four-wheel vehicle would travel. This spot is referred to as the left or right 'tire track'. It is considered the best position for keeping a safe distance from other vehicles, for seeing and being seen and for the smoothest road surface with the best traction. It is also called the 'blocking position' because it blocks or discourages other drivers from trying to squeeze past you in the same lane.

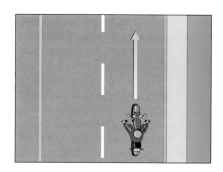

Wrong position

The centre of the lane is not a good driving position because it is coated with oil from other vehicles and gets slippery when wet.

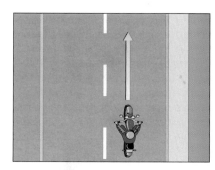

Curb lane

In the right lane of a two-lane road, you should be slightly to the left of the centre of the lane in the left tire track. This position provides good visibility and blocks other vehicles from pulling up beside you in the lane.

Passing lane

In the passing lane, you should be slightly to the right of the centre of the lane in the right tire track. This provides good visibility and blocks other vehicles from driving beside you in the lane.

Centre lane

On a freeway with three or more lanes, do not drive in the centre lane, if possible, because you do not have a blocking position.

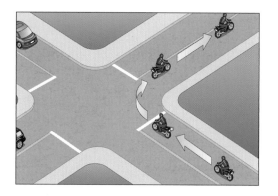

Right turn — same size lane

Approaching an intersection where the curb lane remains the same size, stay in the normal blocking position (left tire track). Some motorcycle drivers angle their motorcycles across the lane (45 degrees) to create a larger blocking position and to make themselves more visible to drivers behind them. Make your turn and move to the correct lane position after completing the turn.

Right turn — wider lane

It is more complicated when approaching an intersection where the lane opens up. Because the stop line is further out, you must move over from your normal blocking position (left tire track) to prevent another vehicle from coming up on the inside on the wider part of the road. Check over your shoulder and move over to the right tire track. Again, you may want to angle your motorcycle across the lane to make yourself more visible and to keep other vehicles from pulling up beside you. Make your right turn and then make another shoulder check and move back to the proper blocking position (left tire track).

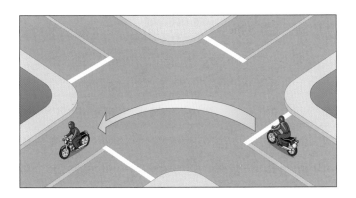

Left turn — from curb lane to curb lane
From the curb lane, make your turn, keeping your blocking position (left tire track) throughout the turn.

Left turn — from passing lane to passing lane
From the passing lane, make your turn, keeping your blocking position (right tire track) throughout the turn.

Changing lanes

Weaving in and out of heavy traffic is dangerous and is usually done by inexperienced or aggressive drivers. When you are travelling in heavy traffic, stay in the same lane as much as possible.

When you have to change lanes, check your mirrors to make sure there is no traffic overtaking you. If it is safe, signal, check your mirror again and then turn your head and check over your shoulder before changing lanes. Checking over your shoulder is the only sure way to see a vehicle behind you in the next lane. This is particularly important because there is little chance a driver in the next lane can react quickly enough to avoid you once you have started to change lanes.

On a road with several lanes, check the far lanes as well as the one next to you. Another driver may be headed for the same space you are.

Lane sharing

Motorcycles and other vehicles each need a full lane to operate safely. Motorcycle drivers should not share lanes with other vehicles. The best way to stop lane sharing is to keep your blocking position, especially in situations where other drivers might be tempted to squeeze by you. This is most likely to happen in the following situations:
- Heavy bumper-to-bumper traffic.
- When you are preparing to turn at an intersection, enter an exit lane or leave the freeway.
- When another driver wants to pass you.

Lane splitting

In heavy traffic, some motorcycle drivers try 'lane splitting' by driving on the line between lanes of traffic. This is extremely dangerous. Do not do it. It puts you too close to other vehicles and where other drivers do not expect a motorcycle to be. Just a small movement, such as a vehicle starting to change lanes or a door opening, can cause a collision because there is no place else for you to go.

Passing on the shoulder

The only time you may drive on the right shoulder of the road is to pass a vehicle turning left and only if the shoulder is paved. You may not pass on the left shoulder, whether it is paved or not.

DEALING WITH PARTICULAR SITUATIONS

This chapter tells you how to deal with particular driving situations you will encounter. This includes freeway driving and driving at night and in bad weather. It gives you tips for driving on dangerous and difficult surfaces, driving in a group and carrying passengers or cargo.

Starting on a hill

Starting on a hill is more difficult than on level ground. Follow these steps to avoid stalling or rolling backward when starting on a hill:

- Use the front brake to hold the motorcycle while you start the engine and shift into first gear.
- Change to the foot brake to hold the motorcycle while you operate the throttle with your right hand.
- Twist the throttle a little bit for more power.
- Release the clutch gradually. If you release it too quickly, the front wheel may lift off the ground or the engine may stall or both.
- Release the foot brake when the clutch begins to engage.

Vehicles turning left in front of you

One of the most common causes of collisions between motorcycles and cars is the car driver turning left in front of the motorcycle. This is because the driver either does not see the motorcycle or misjudges its speed. You can help to avoid these collisions by following these steps:

- Prepare to slow down and proceed with caution if you are going faster than a driver would expect when you approach an intersection with a vehicle waiting to turn left.
- Take a defensive lane position. Move as far as possible to the right to give a little more room between you and the vehicle.

- Think about what you will do if the car turns in front of you. Where will you go? Is there a clear area to swerve? How fast will your motorcycle stop on the road surface?

- Do not focus only on the left-turning vehicle. Pay attention to everything going on around you. Check to make sure there is nothing else in the intersection that could cause trouble, such as another vehicle or a pedestrian.

Freeway driving

As a motorcyclist, you have to be careful not to drive too fast on a freeway. Although it is easy for motorcycles to cut through traffic and speed on a freeway, driving faster than traffic is dangerous because if you drive too fast, you will not be able to react quickly enough in an emergency.

Drive at a steady speed on a freeway. Keep checking traffic all around you and look in your mirrors every five to 10 seconds. As in city driving, your eyes should be constantly moving, scanning the road ahead, to each side and behind. Look ahead to where you are going to be in the next 15 to 20 seconds, or as far ahead as you can see.

Always keep a two- to three-second distance behind the vehicle in front of you. If another vehicle follows too closely give yourself even more room in front or change lanes. Keep a cushion of space all around you and avoid driving in the blind spots of other vehicles. Stay clear of large vehicles. They block your view more than other vehicles and create a strong air disturbance behind them. If you get behind one of these vehicles, the wall of wind can whip around your motorcycle, making it difficult to control.

Entering a freeway

Entrance ramps can be especially difficult for motorcycles. In addition to tight turns, entrance ramps often have slippery surfaces, causing you to drive more slowly than you would in a car.

And because other drivers are usually unaware of the risks faced by motorcyclists, you may have to deal with other vehicles tailgating or trying to pass you.

As you move along the ramp, check traffic in the lane you will move into and find a safe space to enter. Remember to look ahead and check your mirrors and your blind spots. Turn on your signal as soon as traffic on the freeway can see your motorcycle on the ramp. Increase your speed to match that of freeway traffic. Continue to divide your attention between watching in front, checking your mirrors and looking over your shoulder until you can merge safely with traffic. Merge in a smooth, gradual movement to the left tire track of the nearest freeway lane.

Changing lanes on a freeway

Be extra cautious when changing lanes on a freeway. On multi-lane roads you need to check that the lane is clear before you enter it and you also need to check to make sure someone from another lane is not moving into that spot.

Because traffic moves so quickly on a freeway, it is especially important that you let vehicles behind you know that you intend to change lanes. Once you have made certain that a lane is clear, signal early and increase your speed slightly as you move into the lane. Watch to make sure that any vehicle behind you does not speed up.

When passing an entrance ramp where other vehicles are merging onto the freeway, move to a lane as far away from the entrance ramp as possible. This will avoid drivers hitting you if they do not see you and merge into your lane or if they move over to let merging traffic enter.

Do the same thing at exit ramps. If you are driving in the lane closest to the exit ramp, you may be cut off by a driver who does not see you and cuts across the lane in front of you to get to the exit ramp.

Leaving a freeway

When leaving a freeway, get into the right lane well before the exit and signal that you want to move into the exit lane, but do not slow down. Look left and right and check your mirrors. Turn on your signal. Enter the exit lane with a smooth, gradual motion. Once you are in the exit lane, reduce your speed gradually to the speed shown for the exit ramp. Check your speedometer to make sure you are going slowly enough. You may not realize how fast you are going because you are used to the high speed of the freeway.

If you miss an exit, do not stop or reverse on the freeway. Take the next exit.

Driving on dangerous surfaces

Because a motorcycle is balanced on only two wheels, those two wheels must have good traction for the motorcycle to stay upright while driving. Any surface that affects your motorcycle's traction will affect its steering, braking and balance.

Slippery surfaces reduce your control and increase your chances of falling. It is almost impossible to keep your motorcycle balanced on ice or wet wooden surfaces. Avoid these surfaces if you can. If you cannot avoid them, slow down as much as possible before you get there. Pull in the clutch and coast across.

Pulling in the clutch removes the engine drag from the rear wheel and helps avoid skidding. Stay off the brakes. If necessary, use your foot to hold the motorcycle up.

Watch for uneven road surfaces such as bumps, broken pavement, potholes, railroad tracks and construction areas. If the condition is bad enough, it could affect your control of the motorcycle. Here are some tips on handling uneven surfaces:
- Slow down to reduce the impact.
- Keep your motorcycle as upright as possible and avoid turning.
- Rise slightly on the footrests so that you can absorb the shock with your knees and elbows.

Traction on gravel roads is not as good as on pavement. Some areas are better than others. Stay in the tire tracks away from the loose gravel at the edge of the road.

Drive with extra care in a construction area. Slow down; the road could have ruts, mud or damaged pavement.

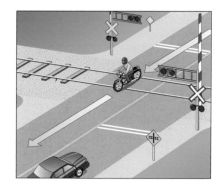

Driving over railroad and streetcar tracks

Remember to check for trains before crossing any railroad tracks. If a train is approaching or the signal lights are flashing, stop at least five metres from the nearest rail. Do not cross the tracks until the signal lights have stopped flashing, the barrier has been raised and you are sure all trains have passed. It is dangerous and illegal to drive around, under or through a railway gate or barrier while it is closed or being opened or closed.

Buses and other public vehicles are required to stop at railway crossings that are not protected by gates or signal lights. School buses must stop at railway crossings whether or not they are protected by gates and signal lights. Watch for these buses and be prepared to stop behind them.

It is not usually necessary to change your path when crossing railroad tracks that run across the road. Be aware of a possible bump and avoid turning or braking while on the tracks.

When you want to cross railroad or streetcar tracks that run parallel to your path, it is best to do so at a distinct angle to prevent getting stuck in the tracks or losing control. Do not try to edge across tracks and do not brake heavily or swerve directly over the track. Do the same thing when crossing other uneven surfaces such as a pavement seam or a gravel shoulder.

Grooves, gratings and scraped roads

When you drive over certain surfaces, such as grooved or rutted pavement or metal bridge gratings, you may feel as though you are losing control of your motorcycle. This effect is greater on a smaller motorcycle than it is on a large one. Avoid overreacting. Keep a gentle but firm grip on the handlebars and drive as smoothly as you can, choosing the best route possible until you get back on a good surface.

Driving at night

Driving at night can be risky for motorcycle drivers. You cannot see or be seen as well as in the daytime. Because of their inexperience, Level One (M1) drivers are not allowed to drive at night.

Another major problem for motorcycle drivers at night is alcohol. Not only are there more drinking drivers on the road to put you at risk, but also some motorcycle drivers put themselves at risk by drinking. Alcohol reduces your ability to control your motorcycle and to anticipate trouble from other drivers.

Follow these tips for driving at night:

- Keep your headlight clean and use your highbeam. Get as much light as you can. Use your highbeam whenever you are not following or approaching another vehicle.
- **Wear reflective clothing**. Also, take warmer clothing and a reflective vest if you are going to be out at night.
- **Reduce your speed, particularly on roads that you do not know well**. If there is something lying on the road ahead, you may not see it in time to avoid it.
- **Use the vehicle ahead to get a better view of the road**. Its lights can give you a better view of the road ahead. Tail lights bouncing up and down can alert you to bumps or rough pavement.

- Increase your distance from other vehicles. You cannot judge distance as well at night. Make up for this by allowing extra distance between you and other vehicles. Give yourself more distance to pass.

Overdriving your headlight

You are overdriving your headlight when you go so fast that your stopping distance is farther than you can see with your headlight. This is a dangerous thing to do, because you may not give yourself enough room to make a safe stop. Reflective road signs can mislead you as well, making you believe you can see farther than you really can. This may cause you to overdrive your headlight if you are not careful.

Driving in rain

Driving in rain can be risky. You are more likely to be tired and cold. The road is slippery, traction may be poor, visibility is reduced and your brakes may be less effective. The best thing to do is to sit it out if you are uncomfortable with conditions. If you cannot avoid driving in the rain, here are some tips:

- **Make yourself visible.** Wear bright colours and reflective or fluorescent material.
- **Have good equipment.** Make sure you have good tire tread, a good helmet and face shield, as well as warm clothing. A one-piece rain suit will help keep you warm and dry.
- **Reduce speed.** It takes a lot longer to stop on slippery surfaces. You must make up for this by driving at slower speeds. It is particularly important to reduce your speed on curves. Remember that speeds posted on curves apply to good surface conditions.

- **Avoid sudden moves.** Any sudden change in speed or direction can cause a skid on slippery surfaces. Turn, brake, accelerate and change gears as smoothly as possible.
- **Use both brakes.** Both brakes together are more effective than the back brake alone, even on a slippery surface.
- **Avoid the worst slippery areas.** Oil from other vehicles tends to build up in the centre of the lane, particularly near intersections where vehicles slow down or stop. Avoid standing water, mud and other dangerous surfaces, such as wet metal or leaves.

- **Watch out for shiny areas and puddles.** Old worn pavement is often polished smooth and is very slippery when wet. You can spot these extra slippery sections if you look for shiny areas on the road surface. Puddles can hide potholes and traction is worse in deep water.
- **Stay away from the edge of the road** when you make sharp turns at intersections or enter or exit freeways. Dirt and gravel tend to collect along the sides of the pavement and can cause you to slide.

TIPS FOR SAFE DRIVING IN FOG

Before you drive — and during your trip — check weather forecasts. If there is a fog warning, delay your trip until it clears, if possible. If you are caught driving in fog, follow these safe driving tips:

DO:
- Slow down gradually and drive at a speed that suits the conditions.
- Use your lowbeam headlight. The highbeam reflects off the moisture droplets in the fog, making it harder to see.
- If you have fog lights on your motorcycle, use them in addition to your lowbeam. They could save your life.
- Be patient. Avoid passing, changing lanes and crossing traffic.
- Use pavement markings to help guide you. Use the right edge of the road as a guide, rather than the centre line.
- Increase your following distance. You will need extra distance to brake safely.
- Look and listen for any hazards that may be ahead.
- Your full attention is required.
- Watch for any electronically operated warning signs.
- Keep looking as far ahead as possible.
- Keep your faceshield clean or lift it up to be able to see out. Also, keep your windscreen (if you have one) and mirrors clean.
- If the fog is too dense to continue, pull completely off the road and try to position your motorcycle in an area protected from other traffic and wait for the fog to lift. If your motorcycle has emergency flashers, turn them on.

Driving in fog

Fog is a thin layer of cloud resting on the ground. Fog reduces visibility for drivers, resulting in difficult driving conditions.

The best thing to do is to avoid driving in fog. Check weather forecasts and if there is a fog warning, delay your trip until it clears. If that is not possible or you get caught driving in fog, there are a number of safe driving tips you should follow. See Tips for safe driving in fog on the opposite page.

If visibility is decreasing rapidly, move off the road and into a safe parking area to wait for the fog to lift.

DON'T:

- Don't stop on the travelled portion of the road. You could be hit from behind.
- Don't speed up suddenly, even if the fog seems to be clearing. You could find yourself suddenly back in fog.
- Don't speed up to pass a vehicle moving slowly or to get away from a vehicle that is following too closely.

REMEMBER:

- Watch your speed. You may be going faster than you think. If so, reduce speed gradually.
- Leave a safe braking distance between you and the vehicle ahead.
- When visibility is reduced, use your lowbeam light.
- Remain calm and patient. Don't pass other vehicles or speed up suddenly.
- Don't stop on the road. If visibility is decreasing rapidly, pull off the road into a safe parking area and wait for the fog to lift.

Driving in cold weather

In winter or cold weather, other drivers do not expect to see motorcycles, even when road conditions are good. You must be even more careful and drive more defensively.

You need to anticipate sudden changes in the road surface, especially if the temperature is close to or below freezing. A road may be cold and dry in one area, but cold and slippery in another. Watch for icy or snow-covered patches, which may appear on bridges, shady spots on the road, windswept areas and on side roads that have not been completely cleared.

Be alert. Generally, asphalt is a grey-white colour in the winter. Be suspicious of black and shiny asphalt. The road may be covered with a thin layer of ice known as black ice.

It is best to avoid driving your motorcycle when you know there is likely to be snow or ice. If you are unable to avoid driving on a very slippery surface, slow down as much as possible before you get to it. Pull in the clutch, coast across and stay off the brakes. If necessary, use your foot to hold the bike up. On a long section of snow-covered road, try to drive on loose or fresh snow. Hard-packed snow has less traction than loose snow.

The other danger of driving in winter is the cold. Cold affects your performance and that of your motorcycle. Here are some things to watch for:

- Cold weather lowers tire pressure. Check it regularly.
- Face shield fogging will be worse in cold weather.
- Probably your greatest danger is from fatigue brought on by the cold. Dress in multiple layers. Keep dry. Do not expose bare skin and be alert to your own slowed reactions.

Driving in a group

If you want to drive with other motorcycle drivers, you must do it in a way that is not dangerous and does not interfere with the flow of traffic.

Never drive directly alongside another motorcycle. If you have to avoid another vehicle or something in the road, you will have no place to go. To speak to another driver, wait until you both have stopped.

The best way for a group of motorcycles to drive together is in a 'staggered formation'. This means the leader drives on the left side of the lane while the second driver stays a little behind — about a one-second distance — and drives on the right side of the lane. A third driver would take the left side, leaving a two-second distance behind the first driver. The fourth driver would be a two-second distance behind the second driver.

2 Seconds

2 Seconds

This staggered formation allows the group to stay close together without reducing following distance and without having drivers drive alongside one another.

Staggered formation can be safely used on an open road. However, drivers should drive in a single line on curves, in turns or when entering or leaving a freeway.

When drivers in a staggered formation want to pass another vehicle on the road, they should do it one at a time. When it is safe, the lead driver should pull out and pass. When the leader returns to the lane, she or he should move to the left of the lane and keep going to open a gap for the next driver. As soon as the first driver is safely by, the second driver should move to the left of the lane and watch for a safe chance to pass. After passing, this driver should return to the right of the lane and open up a gap for the next driver.

Here are some tips to help you keep your group together without interfering with traffic or endangering others:

- **Plan ahead.** If you are the leader, look ahead for changes. Give signals early so the word gets back in plenty of time. Start lane changes early enough to let everyone complete the change.
- **Put beginner drivers up front.** Place inexperienced drivers behind the leader where they can be watched by more experienced drivers.
- **Check the driver behind you.** Let the driver at the back set the pace. Use your mirror to keep an eye on the driver behind you. If she or he falls behind, slow down. If everyone does this, the group will stay together.

Carrying passengers

It is illegal for Level One (M1) drivers to carry passengers. Even with a Level Two (M2) licence, you should avoid carrying passengers or large loads until you are an experienced driver.

Before carrying a passenger, make certain your motorcycle is equipped to carry passengers. Your motorcycle seat must be large enough to hold both you and your passenger without crowding. The motorcycle must also have footrests for your passenger. Without a firm footing, your passenger can fall off and pull you off too. Your passenger must also wear an approved helmet and protective clothing.

Adjust the mirrors and headlight to the change in the motorcycle's angle because of the extra weight. Have the passenger sit on the seat while you make the adjustments. If you carry a passenger, it is a good idea to add additional air pressure to the tires (check your owner's manual). If the suspension units are adjustable, they should also be adjusted to carry the added weight.

Your motorcycle will respond more slowly with a passenger. It takes longer to speed up, slow down or make a turn. The heavier the passenger, the slower the response. To adjust for the added weight you should:

- Drive at a lower speed, particularly on corners, curves and bumps.
- Begin to slow down earlier than usual when you approach a stop.
- Allow a greater following distance and keep more distance between you and vehicles to either side.
- Look for larger gaps when you cross, enter or merge with traffic.

Warn your passenger when you are about to start moving, stop quickly, turn sharply or drive over a bump.

Instruct your passenger before you start to drive. Do not assume your passenger knows what to do, even if he or she is a motorcycle driver. Provide complete instructions before you start. You should tell your passenger to:

- Get on the motorcycle after the engine has started.
- Sit as far forward as possible without crowding you.
- Hold tightly to your waist or hips.
- Keep both feet on the footrests at all times, even when the motorcycle is stopped.
- Lean with the motorcycle.
- Avoid unnecessary motions or talk.

Carrying cargo

A motorcycle is not designed to carry much luggage. Follow these guidelines for carrying cargo:

- **Keep the load low.** Do not pile loads against a frame on the back of the seat. This will change the centre of gravity and disturb the balance of the motorcycle.
- **Keep the load forward.** Place the load over or in front of the rear axle. Anything mounted behind the rear wheel can affect how the motorcycle turns and brakes. It can also cause wobble.

- Distribute the load evenly. If you have saddlebags, make certain the load in each is about the same. An uneven load can cause the motorcycle to pull to one side.
- **Secure the load.** Make sure the load is securely fastened and near the centre of gravity. It is generally not a good idea to tie bundles to the top of the seat.
- **Check the load.** Check the load regularly when you are stopped. Make sure it has not moved or become loose.

Towing a trailer behind a motorcycle

For detailed information on towing trailers, including driving techniques and the special licensing and lighting requirements, refer to "Towing a trailer behind a motorcycle" in the Off-Road Vehicles section in this handbook.

DEALING WITH EMERGENCIES

6

This chapter tells you how to be ready to deal with emergencies that may arise. Studies show that unprepared drivers too often freeze up or do the wrong thing when faced with an emergency.

Emergency braking

Review the section, Braking, in Chapter 3. Practice emergency stops in a safe environment, such as a vacant parking lot, to get a feel for it. The front brake supplies about three-quarters of your braking power, so use both brakes to stop quickly. Pull in the clutch and apply both brakes quickly and smoothly without locking the wheels. If either wheel locks, release the brake momentarily to get the wheel rolling, then re-apply the brakes but not to the point of locking. This is called threshold braking.

If your motorcycle has an anti-lock braking system, practice emergency braking to understand how your vehicle will react. It is a good idea to practise doing this under controlled conditions with a qualified motorcycle instructor.

Anti-lock braking systems, which are also called ABS, are designed to sense the speed of the wheels on a vehicle. An abnormal drop in wheel speed, which indicates potential wheel lock, causes the brake force to be reduced to that wheel. This is how the anti-lock braking system prevents tire skid and the accompanying loss of steering control. This improves vehicle safety during heavy brake use or when braking with poor traction.

Although anti-lock braking systems help to prevent wheel lock, you should not expect the stopping distance for your motorcycle to be shortened. Under normal driving conditions, on clean dry roads, you will notice no difference between motorcycles with anti-lock braking and motorcycles without anti-lock braking.

Some drivers, unfamiliar with anti-lock braking, are surprised by the vibration that happens when they brake hard in an emergency. Make sure you know what to expect so you can react quickly and effectively in an emergency.

Emergency steering

Even a quick stop may not be enough to keep you from hitting something in your path. A vehicle ahead may stop suddenly or pull out and partly block the lane. The only way to avoid a collision may be to make a quick turn or swerve.

The key to making a quick swerve is to get the motorcycle to lean quickly in the direction you want to turn. It takes practice to do this smoothly and with confidence.

Under normal conditions, when you steer, you are actually pushing forward and down on the right or left handlebar to move right or left. This is called push steering. Once you are aware of this push-steering when you turn at normal speeds, you can practice by pushing harder to swerve faster. Being able to do this well can be very useful in an emergency.

Taking a turn too fast

A major cause of motorcycle collisions is running off the road in a turn or curve. One of two things seems to happen. Either the driver badly misjudges a safe speed and takes the turn too fast, sliding off the road and crashing into something. Or an inexperienced driver thinks he or she cannot turn sharply enough and brakes too hard, locking the wheels and sliding off the road and crashing. Inexperienced drivers sometimes crash at speeds at which a more experienced driver could make the turn.

Until you learn the cornering limits of your motorcycle, slow down for turns. Brake before you turn.

Driving over objects

Sometimes you have no choice but to drive over some object in your path. Debris on the road, such as a length of tailpipe, may be too close for you to steer around. Driving over objects is similar to driving over uneven surfaces. These three steps will help you drive safely over most objects you may find on the road:

1. Hold the handgrips tightly so that you do not lose your grip when the front wheel hits the object.

2. Keep a straight course. This keeps the motorcycle upright and reduces the chance of falling.

3. Rise slightly on the footrests. This allows your arms and legs to absorb the shock and helps keep you from being bounced off as the rear wheel hits the object.

It is a good idea to stop and check your tires and rims for damage after driving over an object.

Flying objects

From time to time, you may be hit by insects, cigarette butts thrown from other vehicles or stones kicked up by the tires of the vehicle ahead. If you are not wearing face protection, you could be hit in the eye or the face. If you are wearing face protection, it could become smeared or cracked, making it difficult to see. Whatever happens, do not let it affect your control of the motorcycle. Keep your eyes on the road and your hands on the handlebars. As soon as it is safe, pull off the road and repair the damage.

Animals on the road

You should do everything you can to avoid hitting an animal. However, if you are in traffic, do not swerve out of your lane to avoid hitting a small animal. You have a better chance of surviving an impact with a small animal than a collision with another vehicle.

Dogs often chase motorcycles. To avoid this, slow down a bit and downshift as you approach the animal. As you reach it, speed up. You will leave the dog behind so quickly that it will usually lose interest. If you find yourself being chased, do not kick at the animal. It is too easy to lose control of the motorcycle.

What to do if a tire blows out

If you have a tire blowout, you need to react quickly to keep your balance.

You cannot always hear a tire blow. You have to be able to detect a flat tire from the way the motorcycle reacts. If the front tire goes flat, the steering will feel 'heavy'. If the rear tire goes flat, the back of the motorcycle will tend to slide from side to side.

Here is what to do if you have a blowout while driving:
1. Hold the handgrips tightly and concentrate on steering. Try to keep a straight course.
2. Stay off the brake. Gradually close the throttle and let the motorcycle coast.
3. If it is the front tire that has blown, shift your weight as far back as you can. If it is the rear tire, stay where you are.
4. Wait until the motorcycle is going very slowly, then edge toward the side of the road and coast to a stop.

What to do if the throttle gets stuck

When you try to close the throttle you may find that it will not turn or the engine will not slow down. Here is what to do:

1. Relax and let up on the throttle.
2. At the same time, pull in the clutch and turn off the engine with the kill switch.
3. If the motorcycle does not have a kill switch, pull in the clutch and let the engine race until you can stop and turn it off with the key. You may also be able to leave the clutch out and stop the engine with the brakes.
4. Park the motorcycle until you can get it fixed.

What to do in a wobble

When driving at a fairly high speed, the front wheel can suddenly begin to wobble or shake from side to side. The only thing you can do in a wobble is to drive it out:

1. Firmly grip the handlebars. Do not try to fight the wobble.
2. Gradually close the throttle and let the motorcycle slow down. Do not apply the brakes; it could make the wobble worse. Never accelerate.
3. Pull off the road as soon as you can stop. If you are carrying a heavy load, distribute it more evenly. If you are at a gas station or have a tire gauge, check your tire pressure.

Other things that can cause a motorcycle to wobble are:
- a windshield improperly mounted or not designed for your particular motorcycle
- loose steering-head bearings
- worn steering parts
- a wheel that is bent out of alignment
- loose wheel bearings
- loose spokes
- improper tire tread design

What to do if a chain breaks

Chain failure usually is caused by a worn or stretched chain, which does not fit the sprockets properly, or by worn sprockets. When the chain breaks, you will notice it because you will instantly lose power to the rear wheels, and the engine will speed up. If the chain locks the rear wheel, you will not be able to disengage it, and it will cause your cycle to skid. Try to maintain control and find a safe place to pull off the road as soon as possible.

What to do if your engine seizes

Engine seizure means that the engine locks or freezes. It has the same result as a locked rear wheel. However, there is usually some advance warning of engine seizure, giving you time to respond.

Overheating or a lack of lubrication causes engine seizure. Without oil, the engine's moving parts will no longer move smoothly against each other, and the engine will overheat. The first symptom may be a loss of engine power. You may also notice a change in the engine's sound.

If your engine starts to seize, squeeze the clutch lever, disengaging the engine from the rear wheel. Pull off the road to the shoulder and stop. Let the engine cool. While you may be able to add oil and restart the engine, it should be thoroughly checked for damage.

Getting off the road

If you have to leave the road to check your motorcycle or to rest for a while, check the surface of the roadside to make sure it is hard enough to drive on. If it is soft grass, loose sand or if you are not sure about it, slow right down before you turn onto it. Since drivers behind may not expect you to slow down, make sure to check your mirror and signal.

Pull as far off the road as you can. A motorcycle by the side of the road can be very hard to spot. You do not want someone else pulling off at the same place.

If you need help, place your helmet on the ground near the road. This is a signal among motorcycle drivers that you need help.

KEEPING YOUR MOTORCYCLE ON THE ROAD

This chapter tells you about the rules you must follow for registering and insuring your motorcycle and about buying and selling a used motorcycle. It also tells you what to do to keep your motorcycle running safely.

Insuring your motorcycle

Ontario has compulsory motor vehicle insurance. This means that you must insure your motorcycle.

You must show proof that you have insurance coverage before you can register your motorcycle or renew your registration. If you do not tell the truth about your insurance, or you show false documents, you can be fined $500 to $2,500. You may also lose your licence for up to one year and have your motorcycle taken away for up to three months.

You must insure all your vehicles for third party liability of at least $200,000. This covers you if you injure or kill someone or damage someone's property. Collision insurance to cover damage to your own vehicle is a good idea but not required by law.

When driving your own vehicle or someone else's, you must carry the pink liability insurance card given to you by the insurance company for that particular vehicle. You must show this card when a police officer asks for it. If you do not, you can be fined up to $200.

Registering your motorcycle

Motorcycle registration includes licence plates and a vehicle permit. Licence plates are required for motorcycles when driven on public roads.

Licence plates in Ontario work on a plate-to-owner system. This means that licence plates move with the vehicle owner, not the vehicle. When you sell or change motorcycles, you must remove the plates. If you do not intend to use them on another motorcycle, you may return your plates to a Driver and Vehicle Licence Office.

Your vehicle permit must have an accurate description of your motorcycle. This means if you change anything about your motorcycle, such as the colour, you must report it to a Driver and Vehicle Licence Office within six days. Also, if you change your name or address, you must notify the Ministry of Transportation within six days. You can do this in person at a Driver and Vehicle Licence Office or by mail to the Ministry of Transportation, P.O. Box 9200, Kingston, ON, K7L 5K4, using the change of information stub attached to your vehicle permit.

Buying or selling a used motorcycle

If you are selling a used motorcycle privately in Ontario, you must buy a Used Vehicle Information Package. The package is available from any Driver and Vehicle Licence Office or through the Ministry of Consumer and Commercial Relations.

The Used Vehicle Information Package, which the seller must show to potential buyers, has a description of the motorcycle, its registration and lien history in Ontario, and the average wholesale and retail values for its model and year. It also includes information about retail sales tax.

As well as giving the buyer the Used Vehicle Information Package, sellers must remove their licence plates, sign the vehicle transfer portion of the vehicle permit and give it to the buyer. Sellers must keep the plate portion of the permit.

The buyer must take the Used Vehicle Information Package and the vehicle portion of the permit to a Driver and Vehicle Licence Office to register as the new owner within six days of the sale.

Before buyers can put their own plates on their new vehicle, they must have:

- their licence plates validated.
- the vehicle portion of the permit issued for the vehicle.
- their own licence plate number recorded on the plate portion of the vehicle permit.
- a valid Safety Standards Certificate.
- the minimum insurance required under the Compulsory Automobile Insurance Act.

Safety Standards Certificate

A Safety Standards Certificate is a document that certifies a vehicle's fitness. You can buy and register a vehicle without a safety certificate, but you cannot put your own plates on the vehicle or drive it without one. An inspection station licensed by the Ministry of Transportation to inspect motorcycles can issue a Safety Standards Certificate, provided your vehicle passes an inspection. Many garages are licensed — look for a sign saying it is a Motor Vehicle Inspection Station.

A Safety Standards Certificate is valid for 36 days after the inspection. However, the certificate is not a guarantee or warranty.

Maintaining your motorcycle

Motorcycles require more maintenance than cars. It is important that you read your owner's manual, inspect your motorcycle carefully and fix things right away. In addition to the check you do each time you drive (See Chapter 2), here are some things you should check each week:

- **Tires.** Your tire tread should be at least 1.5 millimetres deep. If the tread is getting low, buy new tires. Inadequate tread depth will greatly reduce your braking traction on wet roads. If the wear is uneven, you need to find out why it is happening and fix the problem. Also check for cuts, cracks, scrapes, exposed cord, abnormal bumps or bulges or any other visible tread or sidewall defect. Also check the air pressure regularly.
- **Wheels.** Check both wheels for missing or loose spokes. Check the rims for cracks or dents. Lift the wheel off the ground and spin it. Watch its motion and listen for noise. Also, move it from side to side to check for looseness.

- **Coolant.** If your engine is liquid-cooled, check the coolant level. At the same time, inspect the radiator hoses, looking for cracks and leaks.
- **Battery.** Check your battery fluid level regularly.
- **Drive line.** Clean and oil the chain and check it for wear. Replace it when necessary. Your owner's manual will describe when and how to adjust a chain. If your motorcycle has shaft drive, check the fluid level.
- **Shock absorbers.** If your motorcycle bounces several times after crossing a bump or you hear a clunk, your shock absorbers may need to be adjusted or replaced.

- **Fastenings**. Check for loose or missing nuts, bolts or cotter pins. Keeping your motorcycle clean makes it easier to spot missing parts.
- **Brakes**. If you hear a scraping sound when you try to stop, or the brakes feel spongy, have them serviced immediately. If your motorcycle has hydraulic brakes, check fluid level regularly.

Accessories and modifications

Making changes or adding accessories incorrectly can make a motorcycle dangerous to drive. Before adding accessories or modifying your motorcycle, make certain that the alteration will not affect the safety and performance of your vehicle and that the alteration complies with the requirements of the Highway Traffic Act. If you are not sure, check with the manufacturer of your motorcycle.

Extended forks. Some drivers install longer than standard forks for styling. However, they reduce steering precision and increase stress on the motorcycle frame and steering components.

Road race handlebars. Extra low clamp-on handlebars make it harder to do proper shoulder checks and may cause discomfort and fatigue.

Touring modifications. Improperly designed or installed fairings, luggage attachments and containers may overload the motorcycle, change its handling characteristics or cause a tire blowout.

CHOOSING A MOTORCYCLE SAFETY COURSE

Every new driver, or those wishing to improve their skills, should take a motorcycle training course. If you pass an approved motorcycle safety course, you can reduce the time you must spend at Level Two by four months. A course may also offer the following:

- personal instruction from experts
- a motorcycle provided for about 14 hours of practice
- your Level One or Level Two driving test
- valuable tips and skills to keep you safe on the road
- the possibility of an insurance discount on your motorcycle (check with your insurance company)

If you would like more information about motorcycle driver training, or a course being held near you, call your local community college, local Driver Examination Centre, or this toll-free number: 1-800-267-6292.

THE LEVEL ONE ROAD TEST

Statistics show that new drivers of all ages are far more likely to be involved in serious or fatal collisions than experienced drivers.

To help new drivers develop better, safer driving habits, Ontario introduced graduated licensing in 1994 for all drivers applying for their first car or motorcycle licence. Graduated licensing lets you gain driving skills and experience gradually, in lower-risk environments. The two-step licensing system takes at least 20 months to complete and includes two road tests.

Passing the Level One (M1) road test allows you to move to Level Two and receive a Class M2 licence.

The Level One road test deals with basic driving skills. It includes a three-part motorcycle skill test. Sets of two cones placed one metre apart, with each set 4.5 metres apart, are used to test your skill in manoeuvring your motorcycle. Following is an explanation of each part:

Walk test

Walk the motorcycle around the cones in a figure 8, preferably with both hands on the handgrips. Without losing control or dropping the motorcycle, stop the front wheel on the stop line at the end of the figure 8.

Serpentine drive

While moving slowly and keeping both feet on the foot rests, drive in a serpentine pattern in a controlled manner.

Straight line brake test

While moving slowly and keeping both feet on the foot rests, drive in a straight line between the rows of cones. Turn and accelerate in preparation for the brake test. Bring the motorcycle to a quick, safe, controlled stop with the front wheel on the finish line.

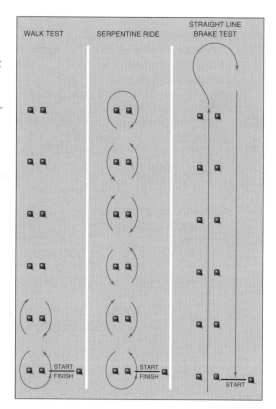

On-road driving demonstration

This illustration shows a typical on-road driving route used at Driver Examination Centres across the province that give motorcycle tests.

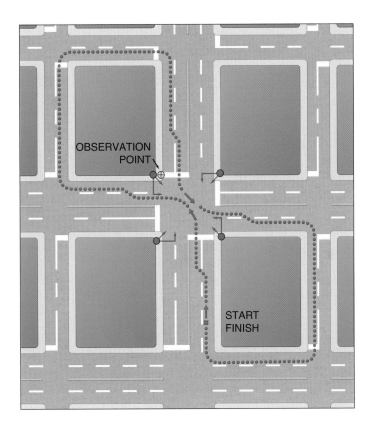

THE LEVEL TWO ROAD TEST

The Level Two road test deals with advanced knowledge and skills that are generally gained with driving experience.

When you take the test, the examiner will follow you in another vehicle and talk to you by radio through a disposable earphone. The examiner will give you directions. As you complete the driving tasks, the examiner will watch to make sure you successfully perform the actions associated with them.

To help prepare for the Level Two road test, this chapter tells you the various tasks and actions that you will be expected to perform.

I. Left and right turns: **The approach**

This driving task begins when the examiner tells you to make a left or right turn and ends at the point just before you enter the intersection. Make sure you take the following actions:

Traffic check

Before slowing down, look all around you. Use your mirrors to check traffic behind you and check your blind spot. If you change lanes, remember to check your blind spot.

Lane

Move into the far left or far right lane as soon as the way is clear. If possible, change lanes before you begin to slow down for the turn. Generally, use the left tire track to turn left from a one-lane road and the right tire track to turn left from a two-lane road. A right turn is usually made from the left tire track of the far right lane.

Signal

Turn on your signal before slowing down for the turn unless there are vehicles waiting to enter the road from sideroads or driveways between you and the intersection. Wait until you have passed these entrances so that drivers will not think you are turning before the intersection.

Speed

Steadily reduce speed as you approach the turn. Downshift into a lower gear as you slow down, but do not rely on downshifting only to slow down. Use both your front and rear brakes. This will also let other drivers know that you are slowing down. Do not drive slower than the speed at which your motorcycle is stable (about 15 km/h). At such low speed, the motorcycle may weave to keep upright. Even if you are skilled enough to balance the motorcycle without weaving, the low speed leaves you with only minimum control.

Space

While slowing down, keep at least a two- to three-second distance behind the vehicle in front of you.

If stopped

You will need to do this driving task if you cannot complete your turn without stopping, either because the way is not clear or you face a stop sign or red traffic light. Remember to follow these actions:

Stop   With both front and rear brakes on, come to a complete stop. At the point of stopping, put your left foot down while still keeping both brakes on. Do not put your foot down until you can do so without dragging it along the ground. Once stopped, do not let your motorcycle roll forward or backward. Keep the brake light showing while stopped. When traffic conditions allow, move forward to check that the way is clear or to start the turn. If you have to stop after you have passed the stop line, do not back up.

Tire track   Stop in the correct tire track to block other vehicles from pulling up beside you in the lane. Generally, use the left tire track when turning left from a one-lane road and the right tire track when turning left from a two-lane road. A right turn is usually made from the left tire track of the far right lane. When you stop, you may point your motorcycle in the direction of the turn to let other drivers know you are turning and to keep them from pulling up beside you. If you stop behind a large vehicle, make sure the driver can see you through a side mirror.

Space   When stopped behind another vehicle at an intersection, leave enough space to pull out and pass without having to back up — about one motorcycle length. If the vehicle in front is a large vehicle, leave more space. Leaving this space protects you in three ways: it lets you pull around the vehicle in front if it stalls; it helps prevent you from being pushed into the vehicle ahead of you if you are hit from behind; and it reduces the risk of collision if the vehicle ahead rolls backward or backs up.

I. Left and right turns: **If stopped**

Stop line   If you are the first vehicle approaching an intersection with a red light or stop sign, stop behind the stop line if it is marked on the pavement. If there is no stop line, stop at the crosswalk, marked or not. If there is no crosswalk, stop at the edge of the sidewalk. If there is no sidewalk, stop at the edge of the intersection.

Turning

This driving task involves your actions as you make the turn. Remember to do the following:

Traffic check
If you are stopped, waiting for a green light or for the way to be clear, keep checking traffic all around you. Just before entering the intersection, look left, ahead and right to check that the way is clear. If there is any doubt about the right-of-way, try to make eye contact with nearby drivers or pedestrians. If it is possible for another vehicle to overtake you while you are turning, check your blind spot before starting to turn. You have not properly checked traffic if another vehicle or pedestrian has the right-of-way and must take action to avoid your motorcycle.

Both feet
Keep both feet on the footrests throughout the turn. Do not walk the motorcycle to ease into or around a turn. You are most at risk from other traffic when turning. Keeping both feet on the footrests gives you maximum control when you need it most.

Gears
Do not shift gears during the turn. An incorrect gear change during a turn can cause the rear wheel to skid. Generally, not changing gears gives you more control and balance over your motorcycle when it is turning.

Speed
Move ahead within four to five seconds after it is safe to start. Increase speed enough that the engine does not stall or over-rev. Make the turn at a steady speed, slow enough to keep full control of the motorcycle while turning, but fast enough to keep your balance and not slow down other traffic.

Wide/short
Turn into the corresponding lane on the intersecting road without going over any lane markings or curbs.

I. Left and right turns: **Completing the turn**

This driving task completes the turn. It begins when you enter the intersecting road and ends when you return to normal traffic speed. Take the following actions:

Lane

End your turn in the lane that corresponds to the lane you turned from. Generally, you should end the turn in the left tire track. If you are turning left onto a multi-lane road, return to normal traffic speed and move into the curb lane when it is safe to do so. If you are turning right onto a road where the right lane is blocked with parked vehicles or cannot be used for other reasons, move directly to the next available lane.

Traffic check

As you return to normal traffic speed, check your mirrors to become aware of the traffic situation on the new road.

Speed

Return to normal traffic speed by accelerating smoothly to blend with the traffic around you. In light traffic, accelerate moderately. In heavier traffic, you may have to accelerate more quickly. Shift gears as you increase speed.

Cancel signal

Turn off your signal if it does not work automatically.

II. Stop intersection: **The approach**

This driving task is done at intersections where you must come to a stop. It begins at the point where you can see the intersection and ends just before you enter the intersection. Be sure to follow these actions:

Traffic check   Before slowing down, look all around you. Check your mirrors and your blind spots.

Speed   Steadily reduce speed as you approach the intersection. Downshift into a lower gear as you slow down, but do not rely on downshifting only to slow down. Use both your front and rear brakes. This will also let other drivers know that you are slowing down. Do not drive slower than the speed at which your motorcycle is stable (about 15 km/h). At such low speed, the motorcycle may weave to keep upright. Even if you are skilled enough to balance the motorcycle without weaving, the low speed leaves you with only minimum control.

Space   While slowing down, keep at least a two-to three-second distance behind the vehicle in front of you.

II. Stop intersection: **The stop**

This driving task includes the actions you take while stopped and waiting to move through the intersection. Remember these points:

Stop

With both front and rear brakes on, come to a complete stop. At the point of stopping, put your left foot down **while still keeping both brakes on.** Do not put your foot down until you can do so without dragging it along the ground. Once stopped, do not let your motorcycle roll forward or backward. Keep the brake light showing while stopped. When traffic conditions allow, move forward to check that the way is clear or to start across the intersection. If you have to stop after you have passed the stop line, do not back up.

Tire track

Stop in the correct tire track to block other vehicles from pulling up beside you in the lane. Generally, this will be the same one you used when approaching the intersection. However, if you stop behind a large vehicle, make sure the driver can see you through a side mirror.

Space

When stopped behind another vehicle at an intersection, leave enough space to pull out and pass without having to back up — about one motorcycle length. If the vehicle in front is a large vehicle, leave more space. Leaving this space protects you in three ways: it lets you pull around the vehicle in front if it stalls; it helps prevent you from being pushed into the vehicle ahead of you if you are hit from behind; and it reduces the risk of collision if the vehicle ahead rolls backward or backs up.

Stop line

If you are the first vehicle approaching an intersection with a red light or stop sign, stop behind the stop line if it is marked on the pavement. If there is no stop line, stop at the crosswalk, marked or not. If there is no crosswalk, stop at the edge of the sidewalk. If there is no sidewalk, stop at the edge of the intersection. Stop in a position where other vehicles cannot pull up beside you in the lane.

Driving through

This task includes the actions you take as you drive through the intersection and return to normal traffic speed. Be sure to follow these actions:

Traffic check If you are stopped, waiting for a green light or the way to be clear, keep checking traffic all around you. Just before entering the intersection, look left, ahead and right to check that the way is clear. If there is any doubt about the right-of-way, try to make eye contact with nearby drivers or pedestrians. You have not properly checked traffic if another vehicle or pedestrian has the right-of-way and must take action to avoid your motorcycle.

Gears Do not shift gears crossing the intersection. If you need to, you may shift gears immediately after your motorcycle is moving but before it is well into the intersection. You may also shift gears in an intersection wider than four lanes if not doing so would slow down other traffic. Generally, not changing gears gives you more control over your motorcycle.

Traffic check As you return to normal traffic speed, check your mirrors to become aware of the traffic situation after you have gone through the intersection.

Speed Move ahead within four to five seconds after it is safe to start. Return to normal traffic speed by accelerating smoothly to blend with the traffic around you. In light traffic, accelerate moderately. In heavier traffic, you may have to accelerate more quickly. Shift gears as you increase speed.

III. Through intersection: The approach

This driving task is done at intersections where you may not need to stop. It begins at the point where you can see the intersection and ends just before the entrance to the intersection. Remember to do the following:

Traffic check   As you approach the intersection, look left and right for traffic on the intersecting road. If you have to slow down for the intersection, check your mirrors for traffic behind you.

Speed   Keep at the same speed as you go through the intersection unless there is a chance traffic may cross the intersection in front of you. If so, slow down and be ready to stop. Watch for pedestrians about to cross the intersection and vehicles edging into the intersection or approaching at higher speeds. Steadily reduce speed as you approach the intersection. Downshift into a lower gear as you slow down, but do not rely on downshifting only to slow down. Use both your front and rear brakes. This will also let other drivers know that you are slowing down. Do not drive slower than the speed at which your motorcycle is stable (about 15 km/h). At such low speed, the motorcycle may weave to keep upright. Even if you are skilled enough to balance the motorcycle without weaving, the low speed leaves you with only minimum control.

Space   Keep at least a two- to three-second distance behind the vehicle in front of you.

Driving through

This driving task includes your actions from the time you enter the intersection until you have crossed it and are returning to normal traffic speed. Remember these points:

Lane   Do not go over lane markings or change tire tracks in the intersection. If your lane is blocked by a vehicle turning left or a vehicle edging into the intersection from the right, slow down or stop instead of pulling out to go around the vehicle.

Gears   Do not shift gears crossing the intersection. If you need to, you may shift gears immediately after your motorcycle is moving but before it is well into the intersection. You may also shift gears in an intersection wider than four lanes if not doing so would slow down other traffic. Generally, not changing gears gives you more control over your motorcycle.

Traffic check   If you slowed down for the intersection, check your mirrors again before returning to normal traffic speed.

IV. Freeway: Entering

This driving task begins on the entrance ramp to a freeway and ends when you have reached the speed of traffic on the freeway. Remember to do the following:

Traffic check   While on the ramp, as soon as you can see freeway traffic approaching from behind, check your mirrors and your blind spot for a space to merge safely. At the same time, watch any vehicles in front of you on the ramp and keep back a safe distance. Continue to divide your attention between watching in front, checking your mirrors and looking over your shoulder to check your blind spot until you can merge safely with traffic.

Signal   If you have not done so already, turn on your signal as soon as traffic on the freeway is able to see your motorcycle on the ramp.

Space   Drive in the left tire track. While on the ramp and merging with freeway traffic, keep at least a two- to three-second distance behind the vehicle in front of you. If traffic is heavy or moving at such a high speed that it is difficult to keep an ideal following distance, change your speed to get the best spacing possible.

Speed   On the ramp, do not drive faster than the safe ramp speed. While in the acceleration lane, increase your speed to match that of freeway traffic. While merging, control your speed to blend smoothly with freeway traffic.

Merge   Merge with freeway traffic in a smooth, gradual movement to the left tire track of the nearest freeway lane.

Cancel Signal   Turn off your signal as soon as you have merged with freeway traffic.

IV. Freeway: Driving along

This driving task checks your actions driving along the freeway but not merging, changing lanes or exiting. Be sure to remember the following points:

Traffic check   While driving along, keep checking traffic all around you and look in your mirrors every five to 10 seconds.

Speed   Avoid exceeding the speed limit or driving unreasonably slowly. Whenever possible, drive at a steady speed. Look ahead to where you are going to be in the next 12 to 15 seconds for dangerous situations or obstacles that you can avoid by changing your speed.

Space   Always keep at least a two- to three-second distance behind the vehicle in front of you. If another vehicle follows too closely behind you, give yourself even more room in front or change lanes. Try to keep a space on both sides of your motorcycle and avoid driving in the blind spots of other vehicles. Try not to drive behind large vehicles. Because of their size, they block your view of traffic more than other vehicles. Drive in the correct tire track.

Exiting

This driving task begins when you are driving in the far right lane of the freeway and can see the exit you want to take. It ends when you reach the end of the exit ramp. Remember to do the following:

Traffic check   Before moving into the exit lane, look left and right and check your mirrors. If there is a lane of traffic on your right, such as an acceleration lane from an entrance ramp, or a paved shoulder, remember also to check your right blind spot.

Signal   Turn on your signal before you reach the exit lane.

Exit Lane   Enter the exit lane at the beginning of the lane with a smooth, gradual movement. Drive in the left tire track and stay inside the lane markings.

Speed   Do not slow down before you are completely in the exit lane. Once you are in the lane, gradually slow down without causing traffic to pile up behind you. Use both your front and rear brakes to slow down. This will let other drivers know that you are slowing down. Downshift as you reduce speed.

Space   Keep at least a two- to three-second distance behind the vehicle in front of you.

Cancel Signal   Turn off your signal once you are on the exit ramp.

V. Lane change

This driving task begins as you look for a space to change lanes and ends when you have completed the lane change. Remember to follow these actions:

Traffic check

While waiting to change lanes safely, look all around you. Divide your attention between watching in front, watching the mirrors, and checking your blind spot. If there is another lane beside the one you are moving into, check traffic in that lane to avoid colliding with a vehicle moving into the lane at the same time as you.

Signal

Turn on your signal when there is enough space for you to change lanes. After signalling, check your blind spot one more time before starting to move into the other lane. Your signal should be on soon enough to give traffic behind you time to react to the signal. If traffic in the lane you are moving into is heavy, you may turn on your signal before there is enough space to change lanes. This will let traffic behind you know that you are looking for a space to change lanes.

Space

Keep at least a two- to three-second distance behind the vehicle in front of you. If there is another lane beside the one you are moving into, be careful not to move in beside another vehicle or into the blind spot of another vehicle.

Change lanes

Change lanes with a smooth, gradual movement into the new lane. Drive in the tire track that gives you the most space between vehicles in the lanes beside you.

Cancel Signal

Turn off your signal as soon as you have changed lanes.

VI. Roadside stop: The approach

This driving task begins when the examiner tells you to stop and ends once you have come to a stop. Make sure you take these actions:

Traffic check

Before slowing down, check traffic in front and use your mirrors to check for traffic behind you. If there is a chance of traffic or pedestrians overtaking you on the right, check your right blind spot just before pulling over.

Signal

Turn on your signal before slowing down unless there are vehicles waiting to enter the road from sideroads or driveways between you and the point where you intend to stop. Wait until you have passed these entrances so that drivers will not think you are turning before the stopping point.

Speed

Steadily reduce speed as you approach the stop. Downshift into a lower gear as you slow down, but do not rely on downshifting only to slow down. Use both your front and rear brakes. This will also let other drivers know that you are slowing down. Come to a stop without weaving.

Position

Stop as far as possible off the travelled part of the road. Do not stop where you will block an entrance or other traffic.

VI. Roadside stop: **The stop**

This driving task includes the actions you take after stopping. Remember to do the following:

Signal   If your motorcycle has four-way flashers, turn off your signal and turn on the four-way flashers.

Park   Depending on the parking surface, position your motorcycle so it will be stable when the kick stand is down. Shift into neutral, or turn off the engine. Put the kick stand down.

Resume

This driving task begins when the examiner tells you to move back onto the road and ends when you have returned to normal traffic speed. Take the following actions:

Start Holding the motorcycle steady, put the kick stand up and start the engine, if necessary.

Signal Turn off your four-way flashers and turn on your left signal.

Traffic check Just before pulling away from the stop, check your mirrors and your left blind spot.

Speed Return to normal traffic speed by accelerating smoothly to blend with the traffic around you. In light traffic, accelerate moderately. In heavier traffic, you may have to accelerate more quickly. Shift gears as you increase speed. Drive in the left tire track.

Cancel Signal Turn off your signal as soon as you are back on the road.

VII. Curve

This driving task begins when the curve comes into sight and ends when you have gone completely around it. Follow these actions:

Speed

As you approach, try to determine the safe speed for the curve. To do this, look for clues such as a sign that shows the safe speed, the shape of the curve and the type of road you are driving on. Enter the curve at a safe speed. In a blind curve where you cannot see all the way around it, drive more slowly in case oncoming traffic wanders into your lane or the curve is tighter than you expected. If you need to down-shift, do so before entering the curve; do not shift gears in the curve. Not changing gears gives you more control over your motorcycle and reduces the risk of your wheels locking while downshifting. While in the curve, drive at a speed that balances the forces created by turning on the curve. Near the end of the curve, begin accelerating to return to normal speed.

Lane

As you enter the curve, look as far around it as possible. This helps you stay in a smooth line around the curve. If you look only at the road directly in front of you, you are likely to wander back and forth across the lane, forcing you to constantly correct your steering. On a curve with a short sight distance, drive in the tire track where you can see more of the road ahead. If the curve is to the left, use the right tire track. If the curve is to the right, keep as far left as possible while watching for oncoming traffic that might be cutting the curve short. You may also change the tire track you are driving in to create a more gradual curve than if you followed the full curve of the road.

VIII. Business section

This driving task is done on straight sections of road where a number of businesses are located.
Be sure to do the following actions:

Traffic check

In a business area, there are many places other than intersections where vehicles or pedestrians are likely to enter the road. These include entrances to businesses, institutions and construction sites, as well as pedestrian and railway crossings. At these and any other locations, look left and right to check for vehicles or pedestrians about to enter the road.

Mirror check

While driving along, check your mirrors every five to 10 seconds. Check your mirrors more often in heavy traffic or where vehicles are moving at different speeds.

Lane

Drive in the safest lane for through traffic. This is usually the curb lane. However, if the curb lane is blocked by traffic or there are many curbside hazards, the centre lane may be a safer choice. Drive in the best tire track for traffic conditions. Usually, this is the left tire track in the curb lane and the right tire track in the centre lane. Stay within the lane markings. Look ahead to where you will be in the next 12 to 15 seconds for dangerous situations or obstacles that you can avoid by changing lanes.

Speed

Avoid exceeding the speed limit or driving unreasonably slowly. Whenever possible, drive at a steady speed. Look ahead to where you will be in the next 12 to 15 seconds for dangerous situations or obstacles that you can avoid by changing your speed.

VIII. Business section

Space

Keep at least a two- to three-second distance behind the vehicle in front of you. Increase the distance if another vehicle follows too closely behind you. On a multi-lane road, try to keep a space on both sides of your motorcycle and try not to drive in the blind spots of other vehicles. In slow traffic, avoid driving behind large vehicles that block your view of traffic ahead of you. When you stop behind another vehicle, stay back at least a motorcycle length.

IX. Residential section

This driving task is done on straight sections of residential or rural road.
Remember these points:

Traffic check

On a residential road, watch out for entrances to schools, pedestrian crossings, driveways, sidewalks and any other locations where there might be traffic hazards. On a rural road, watch for entrances to residences, farms, businesses and industrial sites. At all these locations, look left and right to check for vehicles or pedestrians about to enter the road.

Mirror check

While driving along, check your mirrors every five to 10 seconds. Check your mirrors more often in heavy traffic or where vehicles are moving at different speeds.

Lane

Generally, drive in the left tire track. If there are no lane markings, stay on the travelled part of the road. On a wide residential street, stay toward the centre of the road away from parked vehicles or pedestrians. Where you cannot see far ahead on the road because of a curve or a hill, drive in a tire track that will keep you from colliding with an oncoming vehicle that is over the centre line. Look ahead to where you will be in the next 12 to 15 seconds for dangerous situations or obstacles that you can avoid by changing lanes.

Speed

Avoid exceeding the speed limit or driving unreasonably slowly. Whenever possible, drive at a steady speed. Look ahead to where you will be in the next 12 to 15 seconds for dangerous situations or obstacles that you can avoid by changing your speed.

IX. Residential section

Space

Keep at least a two- to three-second distance behind the vehicle in front of you. Increase the distance if another vehicle follows too closely behind you. In slow traffic, avoid driving behind large vehicles that block your view of traffic ahead of you. When you stop behind another vehicle, stay behind at least one motorcycle length.

MOTORCYCLE CLUBS AND ASSOCIATIONS

Airheads Beemer Club
For owners of air-cooled BMWs.
403-556-8554

BC Coalition of Motorcyclists
Lobby group for riders' rights.
604-580-0111
bccin@mountain-inter.net

Canadian Association for Safe Motorcycling
Awareness and safety issues.
519-938-9559
kcasm@netmatrix.net

Canadian Motorcycle Association
Local, regional and national organization for motorcyclists.
905-522-5705

Canadian Vintage Motorcycle Group
For enthusiasts of old and vintage bikes; many activities.
905-627-4185

Ducati Owners Club
For riders and fans of Ducatis, British and Euro models.
905-420-3955

Federation of Motorcyclists of Quebec
For owners and riders in Quebec.
514-252-8121

Gold Wing Touring Association
Honda Gold Wing owners association.
905-853-2263 (East)
250-716-1438 (West)

Harley Owners Group
Official Harley Davidson club with many chapters.
1-800-668-4836

Motor Maids
For female riders. All bikes, all ages.
905-458-7337

Ontario Road Riders Association
Umbrella organization for Ontario's motorcycle clubs.
416-255-9984

Virago Owners Club
For owners of the great Japanese V-twin and other models.
819-595-1002 (East)
604-576-0448 (West)

PART TWO:
OFF-ROAD VEHICLES

Introduction

Off-road vehicles, snowmobiles and mopeds are popular forms of recreation for many people in Ontario. They are also necessary for transportation in remote areas and in emergencies. But these vehicles are not toys. If you intend to use them, you must know how they work, how to drive them safely in different situations and how Ontario laws apply to them.

It is important to remember that off-road vehicles are intended for off-road use. Dirt bikes and all-terrain vehicles cannot be driven on public roads, although snowmobiles can be in some areas.

Mopeds and trailers are intended for public roads. However, if you drive a moped, remember that because your vehicle is small, it will be hard for other drivers to see you. You must drive with extra caution.

When towing a trailer, make sure your vehicle is in good condition and is the right size and power for the trailer. Follow the rules for trailering and make sure the trailer is properly attached.

Alcohol presents a major risk to your safety and the safety of others whether you are driving a car, motorcycle, snow-mobile, off-road vehicle, moped or towing a trailer. Drinking affects your ability to control your vehicle and increases your chances of having a collision.

This section of the handbook gives you basic information about Ontario's laws and safe driving tips for snowmobiles, off-road vehicles, mopeds and trailers. As you read, remember it is a guide only. For official descriptions of the laws, look in the Highway Traffic Act of Ontario and its Regulations, the Motorized Snow Vehicles Act, the Off-Road Vehicles Act, the Trespass to Property Act and the Occupiers' Liability Act of Ontario.

CONTENTS — Part two

INTRODUCTION 115

1. DRIVING A SNOWMOBILE 119
   I. Getting ready to drive
      a snowmobile 120
      What you need to drive a
         snowmobile in Ontario 120
      Registering and insuring
         your snowmobile 120
      Wear a helmet 121
      Protect your eyes and face 121
      Make sure your
         snowmobile is in
         good condition 122
      Be well prepared for
         every trip 122

   II. Safe and responsible
       snowmobiling 123
       Where you can and
          cannot drive 123
       Public trails 124
       Do not trespass 125
       Obey the speed limits 125
       Stop for police 125
       Report collisions to
          the police 125
       Do not drink and drive 126
       Practice safe
          snowmobiling 127
   III. Snowmobile
        signals and signs 128
        Hand signals 128
        Trail signs 129
        Traffic signs 130
        Wind chill factor 131
        Wind chill calculation chart 132
        Take a snowmobile
           driver training course 133
        The snowmobiler's
           code of ethics 134

2. DRIVING AN OFF-ROAD VEHICLE 135
   I. Getting ready to drive
      an off-road vehicle 136
      What you need
         to drive an off-road
         vehicle in Ontario 136
      Registering and insuring
         your off-road vehicle 136
      Wear a helmet 137
      Protect your face and body 137
      Make sure your vehicle is
         in good condition 137
      Be well prepared for
         every trip 137

   II. Safe and responsible
       off-road vehicle driving 138
       Where you can and
          cannot drive 138
       Obey the rules 138
       Report collisions to
          the police 138
       Do not drink and drive 139
       Do not carry passengers 139
       Practice safe driving skills 139

3. DRIVING A MOPED 141
  **I. Getting ready
    to drive a moped** 142
      What you need to drive a
        moped in Ontario 142
      Registering and insuring
        your moped 142
      Wear a helmet 142
      Make sure your moped
        is in good condition 142
  **II. Safe and responsible
    moped driving** 143
      Where you cannot drive 143
      Do not drink and drive 143
      Do not carry passengers 144
      Practice safe driving skills 144

**4. TOWING A TRAILER BEHIND
  A MOTORCYCLE** 145
  **I. What you need
    to tow a trailer in Ontario** 146
      Licence and permit 146
      Registering your trailer 146
      Make sure your trailer is
        in good condition 146
      Lights 146
      Attaching your trailer 146
      No passengers 146
      Trailer hitch 146
  II. Safe and responsible towing 147
      Loading your trailer 147
      Starting out 147
      Curves and turns 147
      Slowing down and
        stopping 147
      Passing 148
      Being passed 148

DRIVING A SNOWMOBILE

This chapter tells you what you need to know to drive a motorized snow vehicle in Ontario. This includes age and licence requirements, registration, where you can and cannot drive, safety tips, traffic signs and signals and the Snowmobiler's Code of Ethics.

I. Getting ready to drive a snowmobile

What you need to drive a snowmobile in Ontario

You can drive a snowmobile if you have a valid Ontario driver's licence (any class). If you do not have a driver's licence and you are 12 years of age or older, a valid motorized snow vehicle operator's licence will allow you to drive on trails established and maintained by a recreational organization for the use of snowmobiles. However, you must be 16 years of age or older and have a driver's licence or a motorized snow vehicle operator's licence (not both) to drive a snowmobile along or across a public road where snowmobiles are allowed.

A motorized snow vehicle operator's licence is issued by the Ontario Federation of Snowmobile Clubs in co-operation with the Ministry of Transportation. You must successfully pass a snowmobile driver training course to get a licence. (For more information on how to get a motorized snow vehicle operator's licence, see the section Take A Snowmobile Driver Training Course on page 133.)

If you are a visitor to Ontario and wish to drive a snowmobile while you are here, you must have a valid licence that allows you to drive a snowmobile in your home province, state or country.

You must carry your driver's licence or snow vehicle operator's licence when you are driving your snowmobile anywhere other than on your own property. You must show it when asked by a police or conservation officer and give your correct name and address.

If your driver's licence or snow vehicle operator's licence has been suspended, you may not drive any type of motorized vehicle on or off any roads or in any public place.

Registering and insuring your snowmobile

Before driving a snowmobile, it must be registered with the Ministry of Transportation through a Driver and Vehicle Licence Office. This applies to both new and used snowmobiles. If you buy a new snowmobile, the dealer must register it with the Ministry of Transportation on your behalf at a Driver and Vehicle Licence Office within six days of the sale. If you buy a used snowmobile, you must take the bill of sale to a Driver and Vehicle Licence Office within six days of the purchase.

You must pay a fee to register your snowmobile. This is a one-time fee to be paid by the owner of the snowmobile. After registering, you will be given a permit and a registration number decal to display on your snowmobile. Attach the decal to each side of your snowmobile's cowling or engine cover. It should be placed so that the start of the registration number is between 10 and 15 centimetres from the rear of the cowling. If the decal cannot be placed on the cowling because of the design of the vehicle, place the decal on each side of the tunnel, near the reflector light.

Unless you are driving your snowmobile only on your own property or in an area in remote northern or northwestern Ontario that is exempt, you must have a validation sticker on your registration decal. There is an annual renewal fee for the sticker. Place the sticker in the upper right corner of the decal.

You must carry your snowmobile permit with you and show it to a police or conservation officer when asked.

You must also have liability insurance to drive your snowmobile off your own property. Carry the insurance card given to you by the insurance company for the snowmobile and show it when a police or conservation officer asks for it. If someone else uses your snowmobile with your consent, you are both responsible for any penalties, damages or injuries that may occur.

There are separate requirements and rules regarding the operation of trail grooming equipment. Make sure you know what is required before operating grooming equipment.

Wear a helmet

You must wear a helmet whenever you drive or ride on a snowmobile or on any kind of toboggan or sled towed by a snowmobile. The only exception is when you are on your own land. The helmet must meet the standards approved for motorcycle helmets, or motor assisted bicycle helmets, and must be fastened properly under the chin.

Protect your eyes and face

Always wear a face shield or goggles. A face shield can help prevent windburn, frostbite, sunblindness and watering eyes from the wind. A face shield can also protect your eyes from branches and twigs when driving through wooded areas. Select lightly tinted and shatterproof shields or goggles to match conditions. For example, choose clear plastic for dull, cloudy days and deep yellow for late afternoon when flat light can hide depressions in the snow. Avoid dark tinted shields or goggles, which can restrict your vision.

Make sure your snowmobile is in good condition

Before every trip, check your snow-mobile to make sure it is in good working order. Your life may depend upon it. Do the following:

- **Check the steering mechanism.** Turn the handlebars back and forth to make sure the turning is smooth and unrestricted.
- **Check the condition and tension of the motor drive belt.** Change it if necessary or if you are in doubt about its reliability.
- **Check the emergency switch, headlights and tail lights.**
- **Check the battery solution level.**
- **Check the throttle and brake levers.** Make sure they move freely.
- **Check the spark plugs and the tank's fuel level.** Do not use matches or lighter when doing this and never add fuel when the motor is running.

When towing a toboggan, sled or any other kind of vehicle behind a snowmobile, be sure to use a rigid tow-bar and safety chain. For safety, towed vehicles must have reflective material on the front sides, rear sides and rear to make them more visible. Towing is generally not allowed on public roads except to cross the road at a 90-degree angle. This does not apply to a snowmobile being used to free a stuck vehicle, for any emergency rescue or for trail maintenance.

When towing, use rigid tow-bar and safety chain.

Before you drive anywhere, read the owner's manual carefully and keep it in your snowmobile at all times.

Be well prepared for every trip

Carefully preparing for every trip is an important part of safe snow-mobiling. Check local weather fore-casts and make sure you tell someone where you will be travelling and when you expect to be back. Use the buddy system; do not drive your snowmobile alone.

Take along a first aid kit, a tool kit, an extra ignition key, a drive belt and spark plugs. On long trips, include a compass, trail map, flashlight, hunting knife, hatchet, extra fuel and matches in a waterproof box.

II. Safe and responsible snowmobiling

Where you can and cannot drive

You may drive a snowmobile on your own property, on the private trails of organizations to which you belong, or on private property when you have the owner's permission. You may also drive in public parks and conservation areas, except where prohibited.

You may not drive a snowmobile on certain high-speed roads, including the '400' series of freeways, the Queen Elizabeth Way, the Ottawa Queensway and the Kitchener-Waterloo Expressway. This includes the area around these roads, from fence line to fence line. You may not drive on the serviced section of a road (from shoulder to shoulder) except to cross. When crossing, you must do so at a 90-degree angle.

Except where prohibited, you may drive your snowmobile along public roads, keeping as far away from the road as possible in the section between the shoulder and the fence line. Local municipalities may pass by-laws that regulate or prohibit snowmobiles anywhere within their boundaries, on or off public roads. Make sure you are aware of the by-laws in the municipality where you intend to snowmobile.

You may not drive a snowmobile on railway tracks unless you have permission from the railway track authority.

II. Safe and responsible snowmobiling

Public trails

Ontario's public trails are established and maintained by many snowmobile clubs. They are patrolled by Ontario Provincial Police, municipal police, conservation officers and Snowmobile Trail Officer Patrol (STOP) officers. Some clubs require snowmobiles to have and display a trail permit to drive on their trails. Some other clubs allow their trails to be used without a trail permit. Trails may have signs stating that a trail permit is required. If you are unsure, check with the local snowmobile club to find out if you need a trail permit.

For trails operated by the Ontario Federation of Snowmobile Clubs, you must have and display a trail permit. This includes trails on private property, municipal property and land owned by the government. Some snowmobile trail user groups are exempt from the trail permit requirement. Those who are eligible for exemption and the documents required as proof are included in the trail permits section of the regulations of the Motorized Snow Vehicles Act. Snowmobilers who are exempt must carry the appropriate documents and show them when requested to do so.

For information about trails and trail permits, contact the local snowmobile club or the Ontario Federation of Snowmobile Clubs 12-106 Saunders Road, Barrie, ON L4N 9A8. Phone 705-739-7669; fax 705-739-5005; or e-mail at info@ofsc.on.ca. You can visit the OFSC website at www.ofsc.on.ca

Watch for trail and highway signs.

Do not trespass

You are trespassing if you drive your snowmobile on private property without permission from the owner. You must leave the property immediately after you are told to do so. If you are driving your snowmobile on private property, you must stop and identify yourself when asked by the police, the owner of the property or a representative of the owner.

You may be fined up to $2,000 if you are convicted of trespassing. In addition, you may be ordered to pay damages up to $2,000. Under certain circumstances, you may also be required to pay for the cost of prosecuting. Charges will be laid against the driver of the snowmobile. If the driver is not known, the owner will be charged if the snowmobile was used with the owner's permission.

A copy of the Trespass to Property Act is available through Publications Ontario. Phone 416-326-5300 or 1-800-668-9938. It is available over the Internet at http://www.gov.on.ca/MBS/english/publications and www.e-laws.gov.on.ca.

It is an offence under the Railway Safety Act to trespass on railway tracks.

Obey the speed limits

You may not drive a snowmobile faster than 20 km/h in any public park or exhibition ground or on any road where the speed limit for other vehicles is 50 km/h or less. You may not drive faster than 50 km/h on snowmobile trails or on any road where the speed limit for other vehicles is more than 50 km/h.

Municipalities may set other speed limits for snowmobiles on public roads, trails and parks within their boundaries. Check municipal by-laws.

Stop for police

You must come to a safe stop when requested by a police officer to do so. If you do not stop, you may have to pay a fine, or go to jail, or both. If you are convicted of failing to stop for a police officer and the court believes you wilfully avoided police during pursuit — that you tried to escape the police — your licence will be suspended for a minimum of five years. You can lose your driver's licence for the rest of your life if anyone is killed or injured as a result of avoiding police.

Report collisions to the police

You must report to the police immediately any collision that results in injury to any person or damage to property apparently exceeding $400.

II. Safe and responsible snowmobiling

Do not drink and drive

Alcohol is a major factor in snow-mobile fatalities.

It is against the law to drive a snowmobile when you are impaired by alcohol or drugs. Under the Canada Criminal Code, if you are driving a snowmobile impaired or if you have a blood alcohol concentration of more than 80 milligrams in 100 millilitres of blood (.08), or if you refuse a breathalyser test, the police will notify the Registrar of Motor Vehicles and your licence will be suspended immediately for 90 days. If you are convicted of a drinking and driving offence you will have a criminal record and may be required to pay a fine. **All your driving privileges will also be suspended.**

You will have a one-year licence suspension the first time you are convicted of a Criminal Code offence. If you are convicted of a second Criminal Code offence, your licence will be suspended for three years. A third Criminal Code offence will get you a lifetime suspension from driving with the possibility of reinstatement after 10 years. Fourth time offenders convicted of a Criminal Code offence are suspended from driving for life with no possibility of reinstatement. Convictions will remain on your driver's record for a minimum of 10 years. The court can order a longer suspension if it believes that keeping you off the road will improve safety.

If your reading is less than .08 but .05 or more, or if you register 'warn' on a roadside screening device, the police can suspend your licence for 12 hours. This keeps you from driving until your blood alcohol level drops. You must give your licence to the police officer on demand. The police officer will tell you when the 12-hour suspension will end and where to get your licence back. Meanwhile, if there is no one else available to drive and no safe place to park your vehicle, it will be towed at your expense.

Practice safe snowmobiling

Driving a snowmobile requires the same attention and alertness that driving any other kind of vehicle does. You must have complete control of your reflexes. If you are a beginner, practice until you can handle the basic driving skills.

Learn how to control your balance on turns by using your weight to control your movements and leaning in the direction you want to turn. Position your body on the snowmobile in a way that will give you the most comfort and control for the conditions in which you are driving. On level ground, sit or kneel with both knees on the seat. On uneven or bumpy ground, stand on the running boards with your knees slightly bent.

On hard-packed snow or ice, reduce your speed because stops and turns are harder to make and you will require greater distance to complete them. When your snowmobile is trapped in deep snow, remember to turn off the motor before you try to get it out of the snow.

Driving on frozen lakes and rivers can be dangerous, sometimes even fatal. If you are in an unfamiliar area, ask local authorities or residents about the ice condition, inlets, outlets, springs, fast-moving current or other hazards. Listen to local radio broadcast warnings by the Ontario Provincial Police about ice conditions. If you must drive over frozen lakes or rivers, you should consider using a buoyant snowmobile suit. It may save your life.

Wherever you are driving, always watch for trail and highway signs and obey them.

III. Snowmobile signals and signs

Hand signals

Signals tell others what you want to do, giving them a chance to slow down, stop or prepare to turn. Use hand signals to signal before stopping, slowing down suddenly or turning. Give the correct signal well before the action and make sure others can see it. These illustrations show nationally recognized hand and arm signals.

Right turn

Raise your left arm to shoulder height with elbow bent.

Left turn

Extend your left arm straight out and point in the direction of the turn.

Stop

Extend your left arm straight up over your head.

Slowing

Extend your left arm out and down the side of your body. Flap your arm up and down to signal caution.

Oncoming snowmobiles

Raise your left arm to shoulder height with your elbow bent and motion left to right over your head, pointing to the right side of the trail.

Snowmobiles following

Raise left arm to shoulder height with your elbow bent. Motion front to back over your shoulder with your thumb, like a hitchhiker.

Last snowmobile in line

With elbow bent, raise your left forearm to shoulder height and clench your fist.

Trail signs

Trail signs give you important information about what to do in certain situations. Here are some common trail signs and what they mean. Because trail signs are not official traffic signs, they may vary in shape and colour. Watch for signs such as these and obey them.

Stop

A stop sign is eight-sided and has a red background with white letters. Come to a complete stop.

Stop ahead

Be prepared to stop for a stop sign up ahead.

Snowmobiling permitted

A sign with a green circle means you may do the activity shown inside the ring. You may drive a snowmobile in the area where this sign is displayed.

Snowmobiling restricted

A sign with a red circle with a line through it means the activity shown inside the ring is not allowed. Do not drive a snowmobile in the area where this sign is displayed.

Direction signs

These signs give you information about the direction in which you should travel on the trail. Do as the sign tells you.

III. Snowmobile signals and signs

Traffic signs

If you are driving your snowmobile along or across any public roads, you need to be aware of traffic signs and what they mean. The following traffic signs relate specifically to snowmobiles.

Snowmobiles permitted
Snowmobiles are allowed on the road or highway where this sign is displayed.

Snowmobiles restricted
Snowmobiles are not allowed on the road or highway where this sign is displayed.

Snowmobiles crossing
This sign warns drivers that snowmobiles are allowed to cross the road.

WIND CHILL FACTOR

It is important to consider wind chill factor when planning winter outdoor activities.

Wind chill factor is the combined effect of wind and low temperature which makes it feel much colder on a windy day in winter than it really is. This is caused by the faster cooling effect of the wind. For example, if the actual temperature is -10°C and the wind speed is 40 km/h the temperature feels like -21°C.

You need to be aware of the wind chill factor so that you can dress appropriately. Also make sure that young passengers are properly dressed and that their hands and face are well protected.

The chart on the next page can help you calculate wind chill so you will be aware of potentially dangerous conditions.

Wind Chill Calculation Chart

	Air Temperature in °C											
Observed wind speed at 10m elevation, in km/h	5	0	-5	-10	-15	-20	-25	-30	-35	-40	-45	-50
5	4	-2	-7	-13	-19	-24	-30	-36	-41	-47	-53	-58
10	3	-3	-9	-15	-21	-27	-33	-39	-45	-51	-57	-63
15	2	-4	-11	-17	-23	-29	-35	-41	-48	-54	-60	-66
20	1	-5	-12	-18	-24	-31	-37	-43	-49	-56	-62	-68
25	1	-6	-12	-19	-25	-32	-38	-45	-51	-57	-64	-70
30	0	-7	-13	-20	-26	-33	-39	-46	-52	-59	-65	-72
35	0	-7	-14	-20	-27	-33	-40	-47	-53	-60	-66	-73
40	-1	-7	-14	-21	-27	-34	-41	-48	-54	-61	-68	-74
45	-1	-8	-15	-21	-28	-35	-42	-48	-55	-62	-69	-75
50	-1	-8	-15	-22	-29	-35	-42	-49	-56	-63	-70	-76
55	-2	-9	-15	-22	-29	-36	-43	-50	-57	-63	-70	-77
60	-2	-9	-16	-23	-30	-37	-43	-50	-57	-64	-71	-78
65	-2	-9	-16	-23	-30	-37	-44	-51	-58	-65	-72	-79
70	-2	-9	-16	-23	-30	-37	-44	-51	-59	-66	-73	-80
75	-3	-10	-17	-24	-31	-38	-45	-52	-59	-66	-73	-80
80	-3	-10	-17	-24	-31	-38	-45	-52	-60	-67	-74	-81

Approximate Thresholds:

Wind chill at or below -25°C:
risk of frostbite in prolonged exposure.

Wind Chill at or below -35°C:
frostbite possible in 10 minutes;
warm skin, suddenly exposed.
(Shorter time if skin is cool at the start.)

Wind Chill at or below -60°C:
frostbite possible in less than 2 minutes;
Warm skin, suddenly exposed.
(Shorter time if skin is cool at the start.)

TAKE A SNOWMOBILE DRIVER TRAINING COURSE

If you are between 12 and 15 years of age, or if you are 16 and older and do not have a valid Ontario driver's licence, you must successfully pass a snowmobile driver training course to get your operator's licence to drive a snowmobile. A snowmobile driver training course can also be a valuable refresher for licensed and experienced snowmobilers.

The course takes about six hours and is usually held over three days. It covers safe driving practices, snowmobile laws, knowledge of the snowmobile, maintenance, driving positions, survival, first aid, night driving, trail signs, clothing and storage. It also teaches safe and courteous driving habits and skills to help you avoid collisions and property damage.

The training course is offered by the Ontario Federation of Snowmobile Clubs (OFSC) in co-operation with the Ministry of Transportation and is offered by club instructors trained by the OFSC. For the location of the nearest OFSC member club offering the course and the cost, contact the OFSC Driver Training Office at 12-106 Saunders Road, Barrie, ON, L4N 9A8. Phone 705-739-7669 or fax 705-739-5005. You can visit the OFSC website at www.ofsc.on.ca.

THE SNOWMOBILER'S CODE OF ETHICS

Follow this code of ethics and you will do your part to make snowmobiling a respectable, fun and safe winter recreation.

1. I will be a good sportsperson and conservationist. I recognize that people judge all snowmobilers by my actions. I will use my influence with other snowmobilers to promote responsible conduct.
2. I will not litter trails or camping areas. I will not pollute lakes or streams. I will carry out what I carried in.
3. I will not damage living trees, shrubs or other natural features.
4. I will respect other people's property and rights.
5. I will lend a helping hand when I see someone in distress.
6. I will make myself and my snowmobile available to assist in search and rescue operations.
7. I will not interfere with or harass hikers, skiers, snowshoers, people who are ice fishing or participating in other winter sports. I will respect their rights to enjoy recreation facilities.
8. I will know and obey all federal, provincial and local rules regulating the operation of snowmobiles in areas where I use my snowmobile.
9. I will not harass wildlife. I will avoid areas posted for the protection of wildlife.
10. I will not snowmobile where snowmobiles are prohibited.

DRIVING AN OFF-ROAD VEHICLE

This chapter tells you what you need to know to drive an off-road or all-terrain vehicle that has not been licensed for use on public roads in Ontario. Off-road vehicles are any two or three-wheeled motorized vehicles, as well as specific vehicles, prescribed by regulations, with four or more wheels intended for recreational use, such as dune buggies.

I. Getting ready to drive an off-road vehicle

What you need to drive an off-road vehicle in Ontario

You must be 12 years of age or older to drive an off-road vehicle except on your own property or under the close supervision of an adult.

While off-road vehicles are generally not allowed on public roads, there are some exceptions. (See the section **Where you can and cannot drive**). If you do drive an off-road vehicle on or across a public road, you must have a valid Ontario driver's licence (any class).

Registering and insuring your off-road vehicle

Off-road vehicles must be registered with the Ministry of Transportation at a Driver and Vehicle Licence Office. This applies to both new and used vehicles. You must be 16 years or older to register an off-road vehicle and you must be able to prove you own the vehicle.

The following vehicles do not need to be registered as off-road vehicles: golf carts, road-building machines, farm vehicles and motorized wheelchairs. In addition, off-road vehicles participating in a rally or exhibition sponsored by a motorcycle association with more than 25 members do not need to be registered for the event.

If you buy a new off-road vehicle, you must get a bill of sale from the dealer.

If you buy a used off-road vehicle, you will need to complete a self-declaration of ownership available from the Driver and Vehicle Licence Office where you go to register. When transferring an off-road vehicle, you should get the vehicle portion of the vehicle permit from the previous owner.

You must pay a fee to register your off-road vehicle. After registering, you will be given a vehicle permit and licence plate. You should carry the vehicle permit at all times unless

you are operating the vehicle on land owned by the owner of the vehicle.

If you have a two- or three-wheeled vehicle, attach the licence plate to the front of the vehicle in plain view. If you have a vehicle with four or more wheels, attach the licence plate to the rear of the vehicle.

You must register your vehicle within six days of becoming the owner. If you change your address, you must notify the Ministry of Transportation in person at a Driver and Vehicle Licence Office or by mail to the Ministry of Transportation, P.O. Box 9200, Kingston, ON, K7L 5K4 within six days of the change.

If you are driving your off-road vehicle anywhere other than on your own property, you must also have vehicle liability insurance. You must carry the insurance card with you to show when a police officer asks for it. If someone else uses your off-road vehicle with your consent, you are both responsible for any penalties, damages or injuries that may occur.

Wear a helmet

You must wear a helmet whenever you drive or ride on an off-road vehicle or on any vehicle towed by an off-road vehicle. The only exception is when you are on your own property. The helmet must meet the standards approved for off-road vehicles and should be fastened properly under the chin.

Protect your face and body

Always wear a face shield or goggles. A face shield can help prevent windburn, sunblindness and watering eyes from the wind. It can also protect your eyes from branches and twigs when driving through wooded areas. Wear pants that cover your legs and boots that are high enough to cover your ankles. To make yourself more visible to others while driving, wear brightly colored clothing.

Make sure your vehicle is in good condition

Before every trip, check your vehicle to make sure it is in good working order. Your life may depend upon it. Check the vehicle thoroughly before you start to drive, including the following:

- Check the brake control to make sure it moves freely. Adjust if necessary.
- Check that the throttle opens and closes smoothly in all steering positions.
- Check the condition of the tires and tire pressure.
- Check the fuel lines and connections to make sure there are no leaks.
- Check that you have enough fuel.
- Check that the engine is running smoothly. Make sure the vehicle is in neutral before starting the engine.

Before you drive anywhere, read the owner's manual.

Be well prepared for every trip

Carefully preparing for every trip is an important safety measure.

Check local weather forecasts and make sure you tell someone where you will be traveling and when you expect to be back. Use the buddy system; drive with others, not alone. Take along a first aid kit, a vehicle repair kit and an extra ignition key. On long trips, include a compass and maps.

II. Safe and responsible off-road vehicle driving

Where you can and cannot drive

You may not drive an off-road vehicle on public roads. This includes the area between the boundary or property lines, including median, shoulders and ditches.

There are some exceptions. For example, there are some roads that you may drive an off-road vehicle directly across. In addition, vehicles with three or more wheels may be driven along some public roads when they are being used for farming or for licensed hunting or trapping fur-bearing animals. These vehicles must display a slow moving vehicle sign at the rear of the vehicle.

The roads that cannot be driven along are primarily controlled-access freeways, such as the 400 series. For more specific information, you should read the Off-Road Vehicles Act.

Obey the rules

You must stop if a police officer signals you to do so. You can also be stopped by a landowner when you are driving on private property. If signalled to stop by an authorized person, you must stop and, if asked, properly identify yourself.

Everyone who drives an off-road vehicle without care and attention or without reasonable consideration for other people and property may be charged with careless driving. Other offences, such as dangerous driving and alcohol related offences, apply to drivers of off-road vehicles. When you drive an off-road vehicle on a public road, the Highway Traffic Act offences also apply.

Report collisions to the police

You must report to the police immediately any collision that results in injury to any person or damage to property apparently exceeding $1000.

Do not drink and drive

It is against the law to drive an off-road vehicle when you are impaired by alcohol or drugs. Under the Canada Criminal Code, if you are driving impaired or if you have a blood alcohol concentration of more than 80 milligrams in 100 millilitres of blood (.08), or if you refuse a breathalyser test, the police will notify the Registrar of Motor Vehicles and your licence will be suspended immediately for 90 days. If you are convicted of a drinking and driving offence, you will have a criminal record and may be required to pay a fine. **Your driver's licence will also be suspended.**

Do not carry passengers

Do not carry passengers on an off-road vehicle designed for one person. Carrying passengers changes the weight distribution of the vehicle and limits your ability to shift position on the vehicle for control and stability.

Practice safe driving skills

Driving an off-road vehicle is different than any other vehicle and takes more skill than you might think at first. Be sure to read your owner's manual before you begin to drive.

If you are a beginner, practice driving your vehicle in an open area, free of obstacles, until you become skilled at handling it. Choose ground that is uniform, either dirt, sand or snow. Avoid paved surfaces when driving an off-road vehicle. Off-road vehicles are designed for off-road use and are more difficult to manoeuvre on paved surfaces. When driving, keep both feet on the footrests at all times. Do not try to stabilize a tipping vehicle by putting your foot down. You could run over your foot or leg.

Be extremely careful driving through water. First, check that the water is not too deep. Drive slowly and carefully so you can steer around rocks and other obstacles. Driving fast across unknown water is dangerous. Hidden rocks or holes could throw you off the vehicle and cause serious injury or drowning.

Always use a flag mast when driving in dunes and hills. When driving up hills, remember that you need a running start to climb most hills. Be extra cautious when driving among pedestrians, horseback riders, sunbathers or bicyclists.

Read the Snowmobiler's Code of Ethics (page 134) and follow it when driving your off-road vehicle.

DRIVING A MOPED

This chapter tells you what you need to know to drive a moped or motor-assisted bicycle on public roads in Ontario.

I. Getting ready to drive a moped

What you need to drive a moped in Ontario

You must be at least 16 years of age and have a valid Ontario driver's licence (any class) to drive a moped on public roads in Ontario. If you do not have a valid driver's licence, you must pass a vision test and a test of your knowledge of the rules of the road to get a licence to drive a moped.

Registering and insuring your moped

Under the Highway Traffic Act, a moped is a motor-assisted bicycle with the following characteristics:

- Weighs 55 kilograms or less
- Piston displacement is no more than 50 cubic centimetres
- Pedals can be used to propel the moped at all times
- Maximum speed on level ground is 50 km/h within a distance of 2 km from a standing start

Licence plates are required for mopeds. When registering your moped at a Driver and Vehicle Licence Office, you must show the bill of sale. Dealers of mopeds are required by law to provide purchasers with a certificate that guarantees the moped fits the definition under the Highway Traffic Act.

After registering, you will be given a vehicle permit and licence plate similar to a motorcycle plate. Attach it to the rear of your moped.

You must also have liability insurance for your moped. Carry the insurance card with you to show if a police officer asks for it.

Wear a helmet

You must wear a helmet whenever you drive your moped. The helmet must meet the standards approved for motorcycle helmets and should be fastened properly under the chin. To make yourself more visible to others while driving, wear brightly coloured clothing.

Make sure your moped is in good condition

Before every trip, check your moped to make sure it is in good working order. Before you drive anywhere, read the owner's manual. Use lights, reflectors and reflective tape on your moped to make you more visible to other drivers at night and whenever visibility is poor.

II. Safe and responsible moped driving

Where you cannot drive

You may not drive a moped on high-speed roads such as the 400 series highways, the Queen Elizabeth Way, the Queensway in Ottawa and the Kitchener-Waterloo Expressway. In addition, local municipalities can ban mopeds from roads in their jurisdiction where the speed limit is 80 km or greater.

Do not drink and drive

It is against the law to drive a moped when you are impaired by alcohol or drugs. Under the Canada Criminal Code, if you are driving impaired or if you have a blood alcohol concentration of more than 80 milligrams in 100 millilitres of blood (.08), or if you refuse a breathalyser test, the police will notify the Registrar of Motor Vehicles and your licence will be suspended immediately for 90 days. If you are convicted of a drinking and driving offence, you will have a criminal record and may be required to pay a fine. **All your driving privileges will be suspended.**

You will have a one-year licence suspension the first time you are convicted of a Criminal Code offence. If you are convicted of a second Criminal Code offence, your licence will be suspended for three years. A third Criminal Code offence will get you a lifetime suspension from driving with the possibility of reinstatement after 10 years. Fourth time offenders convicted of a Criminal Code offence are suspended from driving for life with no possibility of reinstatement. Convictions will remain on your driver's record for a minimum of 10 years. The court can order a longer suspension if it believes that keeping you off the road will improve safety.

If your reading is less than .08 but .05 or more, or if you register 'warn' on a roadside screening device, the police can suspend your licence for 12 hours. This keeps you from driving until your blood alcohol level drops. You must give your licence to the police officer on demand. The police officer will tell you when the 12-hour suspension will end and where to get your licence back. Meanwhile, if there is no one else available to drive and no safe place to park your vehicle, it will be towed at your expense.

Do not carry passengers

It is illegal to carry a passenger on a moped.

Practice safe driving skills

Because a moped is small, it can be hard for other drivers on the road to see you. Drive defensively and do everything you can to make yourself visible to others.

Making a turn at a busy intersection can be particularly hazardous on a moped where it is difficult for other drivers to see you. Follow these tips for making safe turns:

- Plan ahead. Do not decide to turn at the last minute.
- Check traffic, signal and move into the proper lane for making the turn.
- Signal your turn well ahead of the turning point and hold the signal until you are ready to start the turn.
- Put both hands on the handlebars when making the turn.
- Complete your turn in the proper lane.

When driving on public roads, you must obey all the rules of the road.

TOWING A TRAILER BEHIND A MOTORCYCLE

4

This chapter tells you what you need to know to tow a trailer in Ontario. This includes licence and registration requirements, as well as safety tips to follow when towing a trailer.

Before you attempt to tow a trailer, consider the size, power and condition of your vehicle. Make sure it is capable of towing both the trailer and the load you intend to carry and that your trailer and hitch meet all the requirements described in this chapter.

Trailers that are towed behind motorcycles tend to be small and specially constructed, but must still comply with all the regulations of the Ontario Highway Traffic Act.

I. What you need to tow a trailer in Ontario

Licence and permit

You must have a valid motorcycle licence (Class M) to tow a trailer in Ontario.

It is against the law to tow more than one trailer behind your vehicle.

Registering your trailer

A trailer is considered a separate vehicle. Before you can tow one on any public road, you must register it and pay a one-time registration fee at a Driver and Vehicle Licence Office. When you register your trailer you will receive a licence plate and vehicle permit. Attach the licence plate to the back of your trailer where it is clearly visible. Always carry your permit, or a copy of it, to show to a police officer when asked for it.

Make sure your trailer is in good condition

Your trailer must be in safe operating condition. If it is not, a police officer may remove your trailer from the road until it is made safe to operate.

Lights

Your trailer must have:
- a white licence plate light
- a red tail light
- two red reflectors at the rear of the trailer, as far apart as possible

Your trailer must have mudguards, fenders, and flaps or be designed in such a way that it does not spray or splash traffic travelling behind you.

You must always ensure that you have a clear view to the rear in your mirrors. The trailer must not obstruct this view.

Attaching your trailer

Your trailer must have two separate ways of attaching to your vehicle so that if one fails or comes loose, the trailer will stay attached.

No passengers

You may not carry any person in a trailer while it is being towed.

Trailer hitch

Use a good quality trailer hitch. It should be securely attached to your vehicle, following manufacturer's recommendations. The hitch-ball should be installed so that, when the trailer is attached and tightened, it is level with no tilting.

In addition to a ball and hitch, be sure to use safety chains or cables, strong enough to hold the trailer and load, in case the ball and hitch accidentally come apart.

II. Safe and responsible towing

Loading your trailer

When loading your trailer, strap everything down, inside, as well as outside, the trailer. Do not overload your trailer. Too much weight in the trailer can put a strain on the wheel bearings and axle and make driving your motorcycle more difficult.

The distribution of the weight in your trailer is also very important. Generally, more of the trailer load should be in front of the trailer axle than behind it for proper hitch weight. About five to 10 per cent of the trailer's total weight should be supported on the hitch, within the weight limit marked on the hitch. Poor load balance can cause your trailer to sway or fishtail. The ball and hitch may also become separated, especially if there is too much weight in the rear of the trailer.

Starting out

Before each trip, check the trailer hitch, wheels, tires, lights, load distribution and load security to make sure they are safe. Check your tire pressure with the trailer loaded while the tires are still cold.

When you start to drive, accelerate carefully. Drive slowly and carefully.

Curves and turns

If you are towing a trailer behind your motorcycle, you may need to adjust your position in the lane to take a curve or turn. Adjusting your position compensates for the width and length of the trailer. This positioning will vary on the size of the trailer being towed. When making any turn, always signal and check your mirrors and blind-spots to make sure it is safe to turn.

Slowing down and stopping

A sudden stop can cause your trailer to jackknife or slide sideways or the load to shift. To avoid sudden stops, increase the following distance between you and the vehicle ahead. Keep out of the fast lanes and maintain a speed that will allow you to slow down and stop smoothly in any situation.

Passing

You cannot accelerate as quickly when you are towing a trailer. You also need more space because the length of your vehicle is much longer with a trailer attached. Before you pass, make sure you have enough time and room to complete the pass. Once you have passed, allow more room before you move back to your lane. Do not cut back into the lane too soon. This can cause your trailer to sway and make it difficult to control.

Being passed

If you are holding up a line of traffic, signal, pull over and let the other vehicles pass. Fast-moving trucks and buses create a strong air disturbance behind them. If a large bus or truck passes you, the wall of wind behind it may whip your trailer to the side, pushing it out of control. When you experience this, do not brake. Carefully steer your vehicle and trailer back into position. A slight increase in speed may help.

Other Official Handbooks for You

Copies of this handbook and others may be purchased from a retail store near you, from a Driver Examination Centre, from a Driver and Vehicle Licence Office or from:

Publications Ontario
50 Grosvenor Street
Toronto, Ontario
M7A 1N8

or by calling
(416) 326-5300
or 1-800-668-9938 (toll free)
(416) 326-5317 (fax)

Prepayment required by cheque or credit card — VISA or Mastercard

The Official Driver's Handbook $ 12.95
ISBN 0-7794-2718-1

The Official Motorcycle Handbook $ 14.95
ISBN 0-7794-2719-X

The Official Truck Handbook $ 16.95
ISBN 0-7794-2721-1

The Official Bus Handbook $ 16.95
ISBN 0-7794-2722-X

The Official Air Brake Handbook $ 18.95
ISBN 0-7794-2720-3

All prices are subject to 7% G.S.T. and 5% Shipping Costs. Please add 12% to your total purchase to cover G.S.T. and shipping cost.

Personalize your licence plates — with two to eight characters, as well as a great choice of colour graphics. Then you'll really stand out from the crowd.

Turn the page to find out more.

NOW THERE ARE MORE WAYS THAN EVER TO EXPRESS YOURSELF!

WE'RE HELPING YOU BUILD CHARACTERS.

Now you've got extra choices when creating your personalized licence plate. We've introduced seven and eight characters. So you've got even more to work with — a minimum of two characters and right up to eight. Just think of the possibilities.

Every personalized plate is one of a kind. No one else can have the same plate as yours.

For more information and to order your personalized plates, call 1-800-AUTO-PL8 (1-800-288-6758).

Or visit our website: www.mto.gov.on.ca:80/english/dandv/vehicle/personlz.htm Or drop by your local Driver and Vehicle Licence Office or one of 60 ServiceOntario kiosks.

Gift certificates are available too.

ONTARIO

BCRE8TVE

— YOURS TO DISCOVER —

ONTARIO

NOWYOURS

— YOURS TO DISCOVER —

Graphic licence plates are a hit! And now there are more than 40 choices available. Support your favourite Ontario sports team, community or arts organization, professional group or university. Or select a timeless icon like the loon or trillium.

For a totally unique look, add a colour graphic to a personalized plate with up to six characters.

So express yourself — with colour graphics and personalized licence plates.

For more information and to order your plates, call 1-800-AUTO-PL8 (1-800-288-6758).

Or visit our website: www.mto.gov.on.ca: 80/english/dandv/vehicle/graphic.htm Or drop by your local Driver and Vehicle Licence Office or one of 60 ServiceOntario kiosks.

Gift certificates are available too.

ADD SOME COLOUR WHERE IT COUNTS.